HOW TO KILL A VAMPIRE

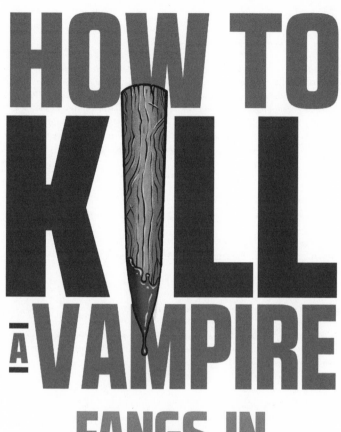

FANGS IN FOLKLORE, FILM AND FICTION

Liisa Ladouceur

ECW Press

Published by ECW Press
2120 Queen Street East, Suite 200, Toronto, Ontario, Canada M4E 1E2
416-694-3348 / info@ecwpress.com

LIBRARY AND ARCHIVES CANADA CATALOGUING IN PUBLICATION

Ladouceur, Liisa, author
How to kill a vampire : fangs in folklore, film and fiction / Liisa Ladouceur.

ISBN 978-1-77041-147-0 (pbk.)
ALSO ISSUED AS: 978-1-77090-429-3 (PDF); 978-1-77090-430-9 (ePUB)

1. Vampires. 2. Vampires—Folklore. 3. Vampire films. 4. Vampires in literature. I. Title.

BF1556.L33 2013   398'.45   C2013-902482-4

The lyrics on page 7 are from "Bela Lugosi's Dead" by Bauhaus; © 1979 Ash/Haskins/Haskins/ Murphy. Published by Bauhaus Music (Bauhaus 1919 Music (BMI)). All Rights Reserved.
Cover design: Gary Pullin
Text design: Tania Craan
Author photo: Dustin Rabin
Typesetting: Gail Nina
Printing: United Graphics   5   4   3   2   1

The publication of How to Kill a Vampire has been generously supported by the Canada Council for the Arts which last year invested $157 million to bring the arts to Canadians throughout the country, and by the Ontario Arts Council (OAC), an agency of the Government of Ontario, which last year funded 1,681 individual artists and 1,125 organizations in 216 communities across Ontario for a total of $52.8 million. We also acknowledge the financial support of the Government of Canada through the Canada Book Fund for our publishing activities, and the contribution of the Government of Ontario through the Ontario Book Publishing Tax Credit and the Ontario Media Development Corporation.

PRINTED AND BOUND IN THE UNITED STATES

This one is for Carol—fangbanger and true friend.

And for all the Lost Boys, wherever you are.

"To die, to be really dead . . . that must be glorious."
—Bela Lugosi as Dracula

"The bats have left the bell tower
The victims have been bled
Red velvet lines the black box
Bela Lugosi's dead
Undead undead undead . . ."
—"Bela Lugosi's Dead" by Bauhaus

TABLE OF CONTENTS

Author's Note

This book is not an encyclopedia. It makes no promises to include every vampire story ever told. I've tried my best to document the key moments in the evolution of the vampire legend, specifically as it relates to how to kill them, with an admitted bias towards my area of expertise, which is English-language horror of the 20th century. Should you find notable omissions or wish to suggest your own favourites, I am more than happy to hear from you. My contact information can be found at LiisaLadouceur.com.

A word of warning: spoilers lurk within. I've made an attempt not to disclose twists of contemporary TV series unnecessarily, but please beware that you're going to stumble upon plenty of plot in this book. And that once you've begun, there's no turning back . . .

Introduction

The Sleep of Reason Produces Monsters; Or, the Vampire and Why It Needs to Be Destroyed

How do you kill something that is already dead? And why would you want to? Well, if that dead thing is about to tear the flesh from your neck and suck your blood 'til there's none left, you might think it's a rather good idea. What? You don't believe these things exist? The undead. Vampires. Of course they do.

Walk into any bookstore, movie theatre, costume shop or toy store and you will find them—those hypnotic eyes staring out at you from countless photos and posters and product packages, looking gothic or grotesque or just plain gorgeous but always with a hint of danger, maybe a flash of fangs. And we regularly invite them into our homes: into our living rooms in horror films from *Dracula* to *Blade* or popular television series such as *Buffy the Vampire Slayer* and *The Vampire Diaries*; between the bedsheets with us on the pages of scary stories by Stephen King and Anne Rice or the deluge of supernatural young adult novels spawned by Stephenie Meyer's gazillion-selling Twilight Saga; sometimes we even let them sit down with our children at the breakfast table in the guise of Count Chocula cereal. We eat, play and sleep with them. We dream about them. We argue about them. We fall in love with them.

They are entrenched in our imaginations, our fantasies and our fears. There may not be a vampire specimen in any natural history museum yet, but, yeah, vampires are totally real.

This isn't to suggest that vampires actually walk amongst us as corporeal beings, lurking in the shadows waiting to bite our necks and drain us of blood. And this book isn't a "how to" guide for those people who seriously believe that they do and want to wage a war against them. Nor does it pretend they are real for the sake of a joke; this is not the vampire version of *The Zombie Survival Guide*. Rather, it's a serious look at a make-believe monster I feel strongly has much to teach us about real life and, especially, death.

The story of the vampire has been told many times. So many times, in fact, that what once was a simple charac-ter—a dead human who rises from the grave to feast upon the blood of the living—is now one of the most complex of all monsters, of all myth. Over time, the traditions of different cultures and imaginations of various writers have brought new (and sometimes contradictory) dimensions to the legend. Some vamps walk in the daylight, others are burned by the sun. Some can shapeshift into bats or wolves or mist. Some can't bear to murder humans for food and so they subsist on animal blood, others are brutal killers. Some are handsome, others, not so much. Some are aristocrats living in castles. Some go to high school. From 15th century Wallachian Gypsies to 17th century Greek Orthodox priests to 19th century Irish novelists to 21st century Hollywood screenwriters, everyone has had their reasons for adapting the vampire storytelling "rules" to suit their own purposes. But there is one thing all these vamps have in common: they are predators that can—and should—be destroyed.

Since it's the topic of the book you are holding, that bears repeating: every culture with a vampire legend has a prescribed means of getting rid of them. No society, when confronted with the threat of a vampire in their midst, says, "Cool, come on in and let me fix you a drink. Would you like to meet my daughter?" And even though vampires have become much more sympathetic and attractive in modern times—to the point that they are now considered suitable prom dates for teens and costume ideas for toddlers, for better or worse—they are still monsters. And monsters exist to be slain.

I don't say this because I hate vampires. I love vampires. I love vampire movies, vampire books, vampire board games, vampire toys. I have playlists of songs about vampires on my iPod. I've reported about these things as a journalist and talked about them on TV. I've written poetry about vampires. I own several pairs of fake fangs, which I've used at Halloween to dress up as a vampire nun, vampire cheerleader, vampire cowgirl, vampire cat, etc. If there were a vampire sports team, I'd be a season ticket holder. If one showed up at my door, I would invite it in.

It would probably be cool to say this fascination all started when I was given a copy of Bram Stoker's seminal novel *Dracula* as soon as I could read. But I'd be lying. Nor did I grow up watching Universal monster movies or all the Hammer horror flicks on late-night TV. No, my first vampire love (well, besides Count von Count, the muppet from *Sesame Street*) was *The Lost Boys*, the 1987 film starring Kiefer Sutherland and the two Coreys, about a gang of teen bad-boy bloodsuckers. As was often the case with horror fans in the 1980s, I was initially drawn in by the poster and its tag line: "Sleep all day. Party all night. Never grow old. Never die. It's fun to be a vampire." I don't know how many times I watched that movie, but I know I never got tired of it. I know that I wanted to be like Star, the film's half-vamp hippie chick who ran with the vampires. I too wanted to ride on the back of motorcycles, live in an underground cave and lure the cute new guys in town into doing bad things after dark. But there were no vampire gangs in my town. So my search for creatures of the night generally happened in the library and the video rental store. And, heaven, was there a lot to sink my teeth into. Tony Scott's 1983 film *The Hunger*, starring David Bowie and featuring an opening sequence with the gothic rock band Bauhaus singing its chilling song "Bela Lugosi's Dead," seduced me. That track actually led me to Lugosi's black and white horror movies (mostly crap public domain VHS tapes I bought for spare change), especially his iconic role in the mighty classic *Dracula*! Between that and paperbacks of Anne Rice's *Interview with the Vampire* (1976) and *The Vampire Lestat* (1985) I was well on my way to obsession. By the time I read Poppy Z. Brite's 1992 debut novel *Lost Souls*, the first book I found explicitly connecting vampires and the goth subculture I also loved, I knew I had found my monster.

Things have changed a lot since then. Vampires are no longer the exclusive domain of the horror genre. They belong just as much to the teens and other "Twihards" who have devoured the Twilight Saga, the "fangbangers" who tune in religiously each week to watch sexy supernaturals take off their shirts on HBO's *True Blood*, and whoever it is that pays to see those action-packed Underworld movies. And that's more than okay. One of the wonderful things about vampires is that they are so bloody adaptable. They work just as well in romance, action/adventure, sci-fi, mystery, fantasy, manga, kids' fairytales, chick lit, westerns, humour, erotica, thrillers, young adult, historical drama, plus any hybrids of these not yet invented. And while I personally prefer my vampires scary rather than sexy (okay, it's actually that I find scary *is* sexy), each time there is a bestselling novel or blockbuster film about vampires, of any style, it keeps the creatures alive for the next generation to discover.

Vamps in popular culture also tend to pique more interest in the origins of the legend. And so academics and other smart types are constantly revisiting the old folklore texts, finding new ways to sell those stories to fans of the contemporary fiction. What we have today is an overwhelming amount of information about vampires— what they look like, where they come from, what powers and weaknesses they possess, et cetera. Therefore I feel it's important, before we get too far along, to set out exactly what kind of vampires I'm talking about.

For the purposes of this book, a vampire is an undead human, someone who either died and then came back from the grave or was transformed in life, usually through a bite or exchange of blood, as originating in eastern European folklore and interpreted by Western culture in film and fiction. I'm not too concerned with the dozens of demons and other spirits with vampiric traits in legends from India, Asia and elsewhere around the world; while some of these are fascinating, I feel that the growing tendency to classify every nocturnal predator with bloodlust as a vampire is misguided, an attempt perhaps by overzealous folklorists and pop culture junkies to beef up their books, or at least make their subjects seem more universal, more worthy of scholarly study. The vampire I speak of needs no such additional validation. You won't find a chapter on Vlad "The Impaler" Tepes, Elizabeth Bathory or other bloodthirsty historical figures who have retroactively been labelled vampires, or any of the 20th century cannibals, psychopaths and criminals who've been called vampires by newspaper editors looking for eye-grabbing headlines—because none of those monsters could be classified as undead. And I won't say anything about so-called psychic or emotional vampires who feed off energy, or the subculture of actual blood fetishists and other "real vampires" who have chosen a lifestyle inspired by vampire habits.

No, there is more than enough to write about the traditional vampire—even if what is considered "traditional" is increasingly fuzzy. I would argue that that is more than okay as well. That the old rules don't matter anymore. A vampire does what its creator, and audience, needs it to do. There's no competition for authenticity between fact and fiction. For fiction (speculative and otherwise) and film *is* our folklore now. The reason why 300-year-old accounts of vampire outbreaks in eastern Europe read so much like a modern horror film is that they are one and the same: a way for human beings to confront their own fears, specifically, their own mortality.

But what of the not-very-scary stuff? Now that you can get toy figurines of these Hollywood vampires at fast food chains, what power do they still hold over us? Do we need to even bother trying to hunt them down, or are they already about as de-fanged as you can get? And what can *Twilight*'s hunky Edward Cullen and his ilk illuminate about our human condition? I offer this: compassion.

The more we love vampires, the more we have to kill them. For how can we continue to watch them suffer? Never seeing another sunrise. Watching everyone they've ever loved die, time and time again. It's a lonely and cruel existence. And it is the modern vampire, the beautiful, sensitive one, whose suffering should move us the most. Yeah, even in the age of reason, we need heroes and heroines to slay monsters, but what if the monster is a lot like us? In becoming enraptured by these vampire-next-door stories, we come to realize that the line between man and monster can be a thin one, that as the very notion of monster has changed it has altered our definition of humanity as well. Vampire or human, all are worthy of our affection, our mercy.

I also think the contemporary vampire still has a part to play in our understanding of and acceptance of our own deaths. In an increasingly secular society, where fewer of us believe in an afterlife, the vampire provides escapism from the harsh reality that we will one day, all too soon, be switched off. What if there was another option? Not life. Not death. But undeath. And not that stinking, shuffling, mindless zombie undeath either. A sophisticated undeath. An undeath that includes love.

The truth is that death is a process, one of decay. There is no simple on/off switch. When are we truly dead? Many people would consider that a spiritual question, about the nature of the soul. But we live in a world where it has become the domain of doctors and lawyers. There is after all a legal definition of death: "irreversible cessation of the functions of the entire brain." That was adopted by the Harvard School of Medicine Committee back in 1968, so we could have things like organ transplants without lawsuits, but it also serves a greater philosophical purpose. This notion of "true death," which appears so much in vampire storytelling, applies to real life too. Death is not one moment in time, nor is it absolute. But it does eventually come. For all of us. And bloodsucking freaks, as extraordinary as they are, deserve it too. I ask you to consider this as you embark upon your crash course in vampire killing, which shall begin now, not with undeath, but with death itself.

CHAPTER ONE

THE EVOLUTION OF VAMPIRE KILLING: A POP CULTURE PRIMER

The Origins of the Vampire

"Sometimes folklore is merely fact that seems too implausible for belief." —*Vampires, Burial, and Death*

Early in the research process for this book, I went to meet with Myriam Nafte, Toronto-based author of *Flesh and Bone: An Introduction to Forensic Anthropology* (2009). I wanted to understand more about the scientific, physical side of staking hearts, chopping off heads and some of the other ways to kill alleged vampires. Afterwards, we got to talking about the definition of death.

In her book, Nafte describes the two types of deaths that forensic anthropologists deal with: somatic and cellular. Somatic death is when cardiac activity ceases—we stop breathing and moving, there are no more reflexes or brain activity. This is followed by cellular death, when our metabolism finally stops and the cells of the body die. I found this distinction fascinating in regard to killing vampires, what we would call in our stories "true death." Because if we look back at the very first reported cases of vampirism in folklore, they had everything to do with these two stages of death, even if they didn't have the scientific language to describe it as such. Take for example two of the most famous early historical "vampire" reports, both from Serbia in the early 1700s.

In 1725, a farmer named Peter Plogojowitz from the village of Kisilova (now called Kisiljevo, in northeast Serbia) died. But shortly after his burial, his family reported him showing up at home in the night. Some versions of the story say he asked his son for food, and that the son was found dead the next day. Others claim he was harassing his wife for his shoes, after which the frightened woman left town. A few months later, nine villagers fell critically ill within one week. On their deathbeds, they reported being visited in dreams by Peter, who they say bit them on the neck and sucked their blood. Panic started to spread, so the local magistrate sent a report to the Imperial Commander, who came to visit and investigate. He opened the graves not only of Peter but all the recently dead to see if, in fact, their bodies had "refused to decompose," which would indicate vampirism according to local lore. Peter's corpse was apparently still breathing, his eyes open and flesh plump, with new hair and nail growth and a mouth smeared with fresh blood. An executioner drove a stake through the body, then burned it. As for the other suspected vamps, the villagers simply put garlic in their graves and reburied them, as a precaution. We know all of this because an official report was made by the Imperial Officer of Grandika and the story later reported in *Lettres Juives* by the Marquis d'Argens, which was translated into English in 1729.

Arnold Paole was a soldier in the Serbian army who believed he was cursed by a vampire. In the spring of 1727, he returned to his hometown of Medvedja (which is not very far away from Kisilova). He told his fiancée that while he was away fighting he had been bitten by a vampire, but he assured her that he had killed the creature in its grave, then eaten some of the dirt and bathed in its blood to ward off any further attack. A week later, Paole fell from a hay-wagon, broke his neck and died. But soon locals reported seeing him wandering around at night. Forty days after he was buried, town leaders decided to dig up his body. A report of the incident reads as follows:

> They found that he was complete and undecayed, and that fresh blood had flowed from his eyes, nose, mouth and ears; that the shirt and the coffin were completely bloody; that the old nails on his hands and feet, along with the skin, had fallen off and that new ones had grown; and since they saw from this that he was a true vampire, they drove a stake through his heart, according to their custom, whereby he gave an audible groan and bled copiously. Thereupon they burned the body to ashes and threw those in the grave.

The sensational incident was not actually reported at the time but rather five years later, when Johannes Fluchinger, a field surgeon, was dispatched to Medvedja to investigate a new vampire panic. After a series of sudden, mysterious deaths in the town, a young woman had reported being accosted in the night by one of the recently deceased. No less than the Austrian emperor himself ordered an enquiry, so Fluchinger came to dig up the dirt, literally and figuratively. After exhuming 40 graves, he determined 17 of these contained vampires. Locals told him the story of Paole, and he theorized that these new vampires had eaten meat from animals that Paole had bitten back before he had been staked. Fluchinger's report of both incidents, published in 1732, became a bestseller, making Paole famous throughout Europe.

A vampire panic often followed a sudden outbreak of death and disease. Not only in 18th century Serbia, but across Hungary, Russia, Greece and most of Europe, eventually crossing with emigrants over to North America where, in the 1880s, vampire hysteria took hold of New England. One widely told tale involves the Brown family of Exeter, Rhode Island. In 1883, mother Mary died of consumption, an infectious disease with symptoms of fever, nightmares, weight loss and coughing up of blood; we now call this tuberculosis and fight it with antibiotics. But at the time it was a mysterious illness suspected to have occult ties. Six months later, Mary's oldest daughter (also named Mary) died and, a few years after that, two more of her children, Edwin and Mercy, caught the disease. When Mercy died, the father and neighbours decided vampires must be involved; they exhumed the bodies of all the dead Browns and found Mercy's to be healthy and full of blood, thereby concluding she must be a vampire. Her heart was cut out and burned. The ashes were dissolved into medicine and fed to Edwin. He died anyway. (You can still visit Mercy's grave in Chestnut Hill Baptist Church cemetery in Exeter. And for many more reports such as these, I recommend the exhaustively comprehensive book *The Vampire, His Kith and Kin* by English scholar Montague Summers, originally published in 1928 and widely reprinted since.)

These cases have several things in common, and in them we see the template for the vampire clearly outlined. A group of people from the same family or village get sick and die quickly. One of the recently deceased appears before his surviving loved ones or neighbours in the night.

Distress ensues. More illness and death follows suit, which raises suspicion that the deceased has, in fact, become a vampire and is draining the living for subsistence. The grave of the suspected vampire is exhumed and the corpse found not to be in a "normal" state of decay; rather, it exhibits signs of fresh blood in its mouth or digestive system, or new growth of skin and hair. Action is taken to "kill" the vampire in its grave to protect the community from any further harm.

You'll notice a significant difference between the folkloric vampire and our modern ones: it is never caught in the act. There is no bedroom bloodsucking, no intervention, no chase scene, no hand-to-hand combat—just rumours of ghastly apparitions, then someone standing over a silent, rotting corpse hammering a stake into its heart. The folkloric vampire doesn't actually *do* anything. This might not seem all that exciting now that vamps have dramatic superpowers like invisibility, hypnotism, flight, shapeshifting, regeneration of body parts and such. But back when the plague was the biggest, baddest threat around, the mere suggestion of a contagion in town in the form of a vampire was more than enough excitement.

In his 1988 book *Vampires, Burial, and Death: Folklore and Reality*, American cultural historian Paul Barber shines academic light on the causes of these early vampire panics. What Barber describes is not supernatural, but super natural. Barber examined dozens of documented cases of vampirism, specifically the description of the bodies that were exhumed, and went looking for the medical and scientific reasons why these corpses would have appeared to be still alive. What he then proved was that every characteristic of these alleged vampires corresponds to an actual step in death and decay.

First off: the bloating. Corpses found puffed up in their graves were assumed to be well fed after death. The truth is that bacteria resulting from decomposition naturally produces gas, which can swell the corpse. New skin and fingernails? The result of "skin slippage," when the top epidermis layer detaches. What about a corpse showing no sign of decomposition at all? And the telltale blood in the mouth? Barber quotes from a medical study that explains how the bodies of persons who die suddenly can decompose more slowly than those who had first suffered from a long illness. Also, their blood, which coagulates after death, can sometimes reliquify. But once blood no longer circulates, its movement depends on gravity. So if the body is buried face down, it can pool in the windpipe and eventually seep out the nose and mouth. Who gets buried face down? In olden times, suspected vampires did—the idea being that when they woke up they'd only be able to dig themselves further into the earth instead of climbing out of it. Finally, as for those who heard a vampire groan when they staked it? Well, a dead body can and does burst, as a result of bloating, emitting a disconcerting sound.

So Barber's book demystifies physical attributes of the vampire corpse, but it doesn't address the other part of the folkloric vampire: its nocturnal hauntings. A body plump and bloody may have been all the evidence needed to conclude a person had become a vampire, but the graves would have been left undisturbed had there not been suspicious post-mortem sightings. When you consider that most of these reports came from the wives or mothers of the recently deceased, who claimed their dearly departed was visiting them at night, these visions could be nothing more than grief-induced nightmares.

If you've ever had an intense dream about someone you've lost, you know how disturbing and vivid it can be. But at least when you wake up, you know you've just had a nightmare. In the 1700s, oneirology, the study of dreams, was still in its infancy. Explanations for such things as bad dreams and sleep paralysis were usually ascribed to the supernatural, such as the German "old hag" that presses down on your chest so you can't move, the Scandinavian *mara* spirit that torments sleepers (and gives us the origin of the word "nightmares," in fact) or the good old incubus, a male demon who rapes women in their sleep. As a cause of nocturnal fits, the vampire fits right in, don't you think? Modern studies have actually shown that nightmares are more common in women than men and that women's bad dreams are more likely to be triggered by anxiety and to be about a loved one's death, all of which corresponds quite nicely to the living/dying conditions of families in 16th century Europe and early American settlements, where life expectancy was much shorter than it is today.

When we look at these historical records in this way, we see how the figure of the vampire served an important purpose: it provided an answer to the mysteries of sudden, mass death at a time when contagion and epidemics were not yet well understood. The destroying and disposing of the vampire, usually by a religious leader or govern-ment official, allowed authorities to take action in order to return the community to safety, or at least ease people's fears. And that's where the vampire may have stayed forever, a solitary corpse able to be dispatched rather quickly so that life could return to normal—in modern parlance, the lone rogue—were it not, that is, for the authors and artists who took the monster to a whole other level.

Dracula Has Risen from the Grave

"The superstition of yesterday can become the scientific reality
of today." —Professor Van Helsing, *Dracula*

The first vampire fiction published in English was John
Polidori's short story "The Vampyre," in 1819. England's
Polidori, interestingly enough, had written his thesis in
1815 on the subject of nightmares. And in 1816, he found
himself in Geneva, Switzerland, with the famed writer Lord
Byron, as well as poet Percy Shelley and Mary Godwin, who
is better known by her future married name, Mary Shelley.
The group spent one dark night brainstorming ghost stories—which produced bits and pieces of ideas, one of which
became Mary's classic novel *Frankenstein* and another Polidori
developed into his tale of the vampire Lord Ruthven.

The character of Ruthven (who some believed was
based on Byron himself) became the connective tissue
between the folkloric vampire and Bram Stoker's iconic
Dracula, who would come 80 years later. While Polidori
did incorporate elements from historical accounts (even
referring specifically to Arnold Paole in his introduction), he also created something wholly new. Ruthven is
more than a mindless revenant haunting his own town.
He is a rich nobleman, pale of skin, yes, but attractive and
charismatic, who travels widely, choosing for his victims
beautiful young women. Here we start to see the vampire

as a true seducer, a sexual predator; whatever was implied in the superstitions of dead men returning to their wives' beds is now fully present. And, most important to our particular study, Ruthven is never caught; in fact, he is able to move about in human society, undetected by almost everyone, save for his one rather impotent companion, Aubrey, who discovers his secret too late. "The Vampyre" was widely read at the time, spawned a sequel and was adapted for the theatre, all of which set the stage for a flurry of vampire fiction in the 19th century.

In 1847, out came *Varney the Vampire; Or, The Feast of Blood* by Britain's James Malcolm Rymer, considered the first English-language vampire novel. Varney is more of a monster than Ruthven, with creepy teeth, who stalks and feasts on young girls. This time, the locals are on to him, although he always evades capture. *Varney* is an incredibly long-winded, disjointed read, which I can recommend for scholars only. Much more pleasurable, and even more valuable, is the exquisite novella *Carmilla*, by Irish author Sheridan Le Fanu.

Carmilla first appeared in 1871 as a serial in the magazine *Dark Blue*, then as part of the 1872 story collection *In a Glass Darkly*. It was the third vampire story to be published in English, and the first to feature a female vampire protagonist. The tale is told by Laura, a young woman who develops an intimate nocturnal relationship with the visiting Carmilla, a rather strange girl indeed. *Carmilla* has been dissected to death by scholars for its homoerotic elements as well as its influence on the female vampire story. But what is most significant about Le Fanu's tale for our discussion is the introduction of the slayer in fiction!

Unlike "The Vampyre" and *Varney*, *Carmilla* climaxes with

a successful vampire hunt. Enter General Spielsdorf, a friend of the family on a mission to find and destroy a young woman named Mircalla, who had brought sickness and death to his household. He convinces Laura and her father that Mircalla and Carmilla are one and the same—and a vampire. "I hope by God's blessing to accomplish a pious sacrilege here," says the general, "which will relieve our Earth of certain monsters, and enable honest people to sleep in their beds without being assailed by murderers." In keeping with folkloric tradition, authorities are alerted, an expert is dispatched and official permission given to open the dusty tomb of the long-dead Countess Mircalla Karnstein. The general, a visiting baron, Laura's father and two "medical men" find her perfectly preserved in her coffin—and laying in seven inches of fresh blood!—whereupon she is promptly dispatched, and her ashes tossed in a river.

And so there we have it, the template for the vampire story we are still telling today: a seductive, nocturnal stranger; mysterious illness and death; supernatural suspicions; expert investigations; a heroic hunt; shocking discovery; and finally . . . the vampire's horrific destruction.

The power of the fictional vampire surged dramatically with *Dracula*. Irish author Bram Stoker started working on his classic novel in 1890, and it was published in 1897. While I'd like to think most people reading a book about vampires have some knowledge of the most famous tale of the monster, the story is well over 100 years old, so the plot is worth a refresher. As recounted in a series of letters, diary entries, telegrams and such, *Dracula* is the story of the Transylvanian Count Dracula and the men and women who come to discover he is a bloodsucking vampire and then fight to destroy him.

It all begins with a train trip: the English solicitor Jonathan Harker journeys to a castle in the Carpathian mountains to meet with Count Dracula and facilitate the purchase of some real estate in England. Dracula is described as "a tall old man, clean shaven save for a long white moustache, and clad in black from head to foot, without a single speck of colour about him anywhere," and he has rather suspicious habits: he doesn't eat or drink, disappears during the day and gets rather upset at the sight of blood, mirrors and crucifixes. Soon, Harker finds himself a prisoner in the castle and, after being attacked by three "sisters" (also known as Dracula's brides), decides to escape. Meanwhile, Dracula has relocated to Whitby, England, via ship. Nearby, Jonathan's fiancée Mina Murray and her best friend, Lucy Westenra, are busy entertaining Lucy's three suitors: Dr. John Seward, Quincey Morris and Arthur Holmwood. Lucy falls mysteriously ill. Seward calls in an old friend, Professor Abraham Van Helsing, who suspects vampirism. Despite Van Helsing's attempts to cure and protect Lucy, the girl is still attacked by a "wolf" in the night and dies. She's back soon though: reports have her risen from the grave and preying on local children. Van Helsing springs to action: engaging the three gents in a plan to track down vampire Lucy and destroy her—which they do. Meanwhile, Jonathan returns with some outrageous tales from Transylvania, then he and Mina (now his wife) join the others in finding and slaying Count Dracula, whom everyone now believes to be the cause of Lucy's death and a threat to them all.

The plot really picks up when Dracula attacks Mina in the night, feeding on her blood and even giving her his own blood, which allows him to control her from a distance. As Mina slowly falls into a weakened trance-like state, the other characters use her new psychic connection to Dracula to locate him. A lengthy pursuit ensues. In the climax, everyone converges on the Count just before sundown, Jonathan cuts the vampire's throat with a knife and Quincey stabs him in the heart. And just like that, the vampire crumbles to dust. But as a presence in our culture, he certainly didn't die.

Volumes have been written on *Dracula*'s influence—on the gothic literature of its time, on the horror film industry soon to come and, of course, on vampire mythology. To learn more about Stoker's classic, consult the bibliography at the back of this book for some recommended reading. Meanwhile, let us focus here on the novel's importance to the development of the vampire's powers, weaknesses and ultimate destruction.

Fully one third of *Dracula* is devoted to chasing down the vampire. Like Le Fanu before him, Stoker incorporated many known elements from folklore, such as using garlic to keep the vampire at bay and the wooden stake to the heart as the finishing move to bring true death. He also created his own rules: a vampire cannot enter a home without permission, must rest in his native soil, casts no reflection in mirrors and can transform into a bat. We know all this because Van Helsing tells us as much. Like General Spielsdorf from *Carmilla*, Van Helsing is the expert from out of town who reveals the truth about vampirism to the other characters, and to the reader. But in Van

Helsing, Stoker created an exciting new kind of slayer—a scientist who believes in the supernatural, a professor with a wealth of book knowledge, a teacher who enlightens others as to the dangers of vampires, and the leader of the charge who wields the appropriate weapons. The fact that Van Helsing doesn't actually stake Count Dracula doesn't diminish him as the grandfather of the vampire slaying figure. In fact, the Van Helsing character has become almost as iconic as any vampire: he's continued to star in other books and films inspired by *Dracula*, to the point that he scored his own movie, the 2004 action film *Van Helsing*.

And so in Stoker's *Dracula* we have both the ultimate villain and the perfect hero. Count Dracula represents the unknown evil, coming from another part of the world, somewhere foreign and frightening and possibly demonic. He is the Other, and yet part human. For underneath his grotesque features, he looks like us, was once us. In his nemesis Van Helsing, we have the slayer as a kind of exorcist. Protector of virtue, saviour of souls. For that, in the end, is what *Dracula* is all about: saving souls. Just as 16th century folk tales about vampires highlighted the anxieties around dreams, disease and sudden death, Stoker's book illuminates the fears of his Victorian era: the creep of modern science and secular thinking, wanton women, invading foreigners. But in the end, good does triumph over supernatural evil. The vampire is destroyed and Mina's purity is restored; she and Jonathan have a child and live happily ever after.

It was all too irresistible.

Ghouls on Film

"Enter the Count." —screenplay direction, *Nosferatu*

The 1931 classic *Dracula* was not the first vampire movie. Tod Browning's *London After Midnight* came out in 1927, snagging that honour. It wasn't even the first adaptation of Bram Stoker's book *Dracula*. That goes to 1922's silent film *Nosferatu, eine Symphonie des Grauens*, which is *Dracula* in all but name. Oh, the German producers changed the character names and some details, but "Count Orlok" is unmistakably Stoker's vampire: a monstrous, bloodsucking "bird of death" who lives in a Transylvanian castle and sleeps in a coffin. He too wants to purchase some real estate abroad, goes on a trip and ends up stalking the visiting solicitor's fiancée in her bedroom. It showcases a truly mesmerizing performance by the German actor Max Schreck, and the striking Expressionist style of director F.W. Murnau has been widely recognized as pioneering in the gothic cinema of light and shadow. (The film would be remade as *Nosferatu: Phantom der Nacht* in 1979 by German madman/director Werner Herzog and immortalized further in the 2000 American art movie *Shadow of the Vampire*, directed by E. Elias Merhige and starring Willem Dafoe as Max Schreck—a kind of meta–vampire film which just happens to be my personal favourite vamp movie of all time, by the way.)

Nosferatu is important to cinema but even more

important to vampire killing myth-making, for it birthed the idea that vampires could be destroyed by exposure to sunlight. In the film's final scene, the sun's rays hit the Count and, in a slow dissolve, the vampire fades to nothingness. This short sequence is the origin of the rule that sunlight isn't just annoying to vampires, or something that weakens them, but that it is fatal, even just a bit of it. This wasn't in folklore. It wasn't in Stoker. It was an invention of F.W. Murnau. His idea has endured as a cornerstone of vampire storytelling, gaining strength over time to the point where the image of a vamp burning to ashes in the sun is now just as common as one with a wooden stake through the heart. The sad thing about *Nosferatu* is that few people saw it at the time. Bram Stoker's widow, Florence Stoker, successfully sued for copyright infringement and had copies of the film confiscated and destroyed. It wouldn't be until the 1970s that found copies were restored and really started to circulate. (*London After Midnight* remains a lost film from the silent era, despite a re-creation of sorts from film stills done by Turner Classic Movies in 2002.) What audiences did see in the early days of cinema, and in great numbers, was *Dracula*.

As with the novel, the story of the film is well known. Adapted from a hit 1924 London play by Hamilton Deane based on Stoker's book (which was itself greatly revised by John L. Balderston in 1927 to suit American tastes and sensibilities for Broadway), the 1931 film, directed by American Tod Browning and starring Hungarian Bela Lugosi as the Count, was a smash success for Universal Pictures. Lugosi, who had already played Dracula on stage, came to epitomize what vampires looked and sounded like:

a nobleman in formal evening wear (including a cloak) with a heavy foreign accent. The screenplay deviates from the novel often in order to speed the plot along, but the rules of vampirism Stoker used, both of his own invention and based on his folklore research, remain: Lugosi's Dracula doesn't like crucifixes or mirrors; he can change into a bat, has hypnotic powers and sleeps by day on his native soil. Van Helsing (played by American character actor Edward Van Sloan) leads the charge against the undead Lucy and master vampire. And here, he even stakes Dracula to death!

Lugosi and Dracula kick-started an entire wave of vampire movies in the 1930s and 1940s. (*Frankenstein*'s English director James Whale was asked by Universal to do a sequel with a daughter-of-Dracula theme but he so loathed the project that he rewrote the script with not-so-subtle homoerotic overtones and insisted that that was the only version he'd shoot. He was given *Bride of Frankenstein* instead.) The eventual sequel, *Dracula's Daughter* (1936), was directed by Lambert Hillyer and stars Gloria Holden as a seductive female vampire who bemoans her fate for much of her screen time and is ultimately killed by her own servant using a wooden arrow. Here we see the introduction of the variation on the traditional wooden stake, where any weapon made of wood can kill a vampire. We learn that anyone can be a vampire killer, with or without any proper authority, as long as they have the tools. Also, the Countess's brooding demeanour (she is dying to be freed from what she refers to as the "curse" of vampirism) provides a newfound angst angle, one which would later influence the works of Anne Rice, who has repeatedly cited *Dracula's Daughter* as one of her favourites. *Son of Dracula* (1943) and *House of Dracula* (1945) mix Stoker and Murnau: in both films, Count Dracula is unable to get to his coffin before sunrise and is killed by exposure.

It's clear that in the hands of screenwriters and directors the vampire begins to take on new characteristics, ones more suited to the medium of cinema. More dramatic. More seductive. More powerful. An entire industry of vampire films seemed to spring up, producing a list of classics and not-so-classics. (In addition to the exploding horror genre, there were many erotic/art house vampire films, vampire sci-fi, foreign vampire films and even vampire cartoons and comedies.) In 1958, England's Hammer Films produced its version of *Dracula*. Retitled *Horror of Dracula* for the U.S. market, it was directed by Terence Fisher and starred soon-to-be acting legends Christopher Lee (now Sir Christopher, if you please) as the Count and Peter Cushing as Van Helsing. The film was the first in a glorious era of gothic horror from Hammer, with Technicolor red blood and, for the first time, a vampire sporting actual fangs. These widely seen Universal and Hammer vampire films meant that audiences were becoming very familiar with the usual plot lines, with the vampire being chased for a while and then finally dispatched via stake or sunlight. To keep audiences enthralled, filmmakers needed inventive ways to confront and destroy the villain for the climax. The showdown needed a money shot. And so everything started to get bigger, and more bad-ass. Why use a small rosary to ward off your vampire when you could have Dracula fall onto an oversized crucifix and impale himself as he does in 1968's *Dracula Has Risen from the Grave*?

It was all great fun, and by the 1980s, vampire movie characters had become self-aware, sassier and much younger. Instead of old professor types from afar who learned their vampire-slayer trade from researching dusty occult books, we now had teenagers who grew up on horror stories, were quick to recognize a vampire and knew what to do about one. In 1985's Hollywood box office hit *Fright Night*, when young Charley Brewster (William Ragsdale) thinks a vampire has moved in next door, he turns to his favourite TV horror host for help (a character based in part on Peter Cushing), but it turns out Brewster is far more capable of taking charge himself. In *The Lost Boys*, it's the teen Frog Brothers, who learned everything they need to know about killing vampires from reading comic books. By the time we get to the turn of the millennium, characters are routinely cracking jokes about garlic and crucifixes. The old tools had lost their power to instill fear in both the vampires and the audience; for the slayer of cinema, it was time to modernize. And so, like Bruce Wayne or James Bond, new-school movie slayers developed high-tech weaponry and fancy special effects gizmos. Blade, a character from a 1970s comic book, took over from Van Helsing as the pre-eminent vampire hunter in three blockbuster films, *Blade* (1998), *Blade II* (2002) and *Blade: Trinity* (2004), starring Wesley Snipes. He's half-vamp himself, a so-called *dhampir*, and a full-on martial artist and swordsman with an arsenal of serious firepower. Nearly a century after F.W. Murnau had the idea that sunlight could kill a vampire, we had Blade packing bullets filled with liquid UV. This was not simply the result of advances in movie special effects (although that

HOW TO KILL A VAMPIRE

helped), but a response to how much the undead threat had changed. Vampires were no longer merely the product of superstition and the supernatural, but also of science. And like a virus, they were spreading fast.

22

Rise of the Planet of the Vamps

"I went to see *Dracula* and the thought occurred that, if one vampire was scary, a world filled with vampires would really be scary." —Richard Matheson

Richard Matheson was right: it is really scary. In the American author's 1954 novel, *I Am Legend*, Robert Neville is the last human on Earth. Everyone else has been transformed into a vampire. It's no longer about killing them one by one with a stake, although he certainly gives that his best shot. No, Neville must find a way to destroy them *all*. In this tale, vampires are not gentlemen with some bad habits. They are not death personified as seduction. They are disgusting, a virus, a plague. With its hordes of vicious undead, *I Am Legend* has often been cited as the origin of the modern zombie craze, but it was also highly influential on the evolution of the vampire from a lone monster sleeping in the dirt, whose supernatural powers can be beat with know-how and faith, to an entire vampire society that cannot be stopped. No longer do *they* walk amongst *us*—there is barely any *us* left.

I Am Legend is a prime example of a vampire story plugging into the fears of its time. Although the story can be, and has been, read as a metaphor for the spread of communism, that was never the author's intent. Consciously or not, Matheson provided horror fans in the 1950s with a glimpse into the future, where the monster was not any one bogeyman, but rather society itself. With medical breakthroughs happening at a rapid pace post–Second World War (for one, antibiotics helped diminish the spread of tuberculosis, so often associated with vampires in Stoker's era), there was less of a chance that you'd die in the night of a mysterious disease. But after the Holocaust, the idea that Hell may be right here on Earth was certainly on a lot of people's minds. Matheson's story set the stage for other American vampire-rising masterworks, such as Stephen King's 'Salem's Lot (1975) and Robert R. McCammon's They Thirst (1981). Whether they were taking over your small town, a massive metropolis or the entire planet, vampire stories played on the fear that there could be an unstoppable force lurking in the shadows, waiting to enslave and eliminate human civilization.

Anne Rice had a different idea. The American novelist also imagined more than one vampire. But hers were not a vicious army seeking to take over the world: they were small, sophisticated clans operating in secret. They were families. The Vampire Chronicles, which played out over 10 novels beginning with Interview with the Vampire, changed everything. It's how we get from Nosferatu to Twilight. Rice's lead vampire Lestat is a cultured, angst-ridden romantic who yearns desperately to be understood, and to be loved. You can't harm him with sacred objects such as crucifixes. You can hurt his feelings though.

Lestat wasn't the first sensitive vampire. In the 1960s, American TV viewers swooned for Barnabas Collins (played by Canadian Jonathan Frid), the tormented star of ABC's supernatural afternoon soap Dark Shadows. (The cult show was remade in the 1990s by NBC and again in 2012 as a feature film by Tim Burton, starring Johnny Depp.) And Barnabas wasn't the only one of his era. Also in the '70s, American author Chelsea Quinn Yarbro created the very popular suave French Count Saint-Germain, based on the real life Comte de Saint-Germain, a 16th century mystic, alchemist and charlatan thought by some to be undead. Yarbro's Count first appeared at the court of Louis XV in the 1978 historical romance novel *Hotel Transylvania*, which spawned an entire series in which the cultured, thousand-year-old vampire was doomed to wander the globe through the ages. Saint-Gemain has had exciting adventures during some of the most important moments in human civilization, but Rice's saga was truly epic, and her vampires uniquely complex. Her creatures could care deeply for another vampire for all of eternity and yet if angered or betrayed would throw their best friends onto a funeral pyre. They also exquisitely portrayed the mal-aise of a thousand-year existence. There is madness in immortality, after all.

All of this caused a seismic shift in vampire storytell-ing. Plus, by the time *Interview* was made into a big-budget film in 1994 starring Tom Cruise as Lestat, there was a resurgence of the gothic in popular culture. The kids were acting out *Vampire: The Masquerade* role-playing games and listening to Marilyn Manson. Haute couture runways and fashion magazines were declaring black the new black. The influence of goth (which is nothing if not romantic, and is particularly romantic about death) was significant on the horror genre at this time. Instead of wanting to slay the vampire, we wanted to *be* the vampire. Dressing and living sumptuously. Drinking blood from consenting partners. Jet-setting around the world. You didn't need to get buried in the dirty ground first and claw your way back out either. Much of the old folklore about who becomes a vampire and how had all but been forgotten. Now anyone could become a vampire and stay young forever, if only you could find one willing to bite your neck and let you suck their blood. And if that sounds like Harlequin, not horror, remember that this shift happened in the age of AIDS, when exchanging fluids with a mysterious stranger in the night was about as scary a scenario as you could get. So in granting us an opportunity to indulge that fantasy from a safe place, the vampire myth tapped into fears of the day, and proved once again to be an important tool for confronting our anxieties around death in a way that let us go on living.

The Slayer, Revamped

"It's my first day! I was afraid that I was gonna be behind in all
my classes, that I wouldn't make any friends, that I would have
last month's hair. I didn't think there'd be vampires on campus."
—Buffy Summers, "Welcome to the Hellmouth,"
Buffy the Vampire Slayer

Around the same time that the gothic romantic vampire
really took off came the rise of a new kind of feminism in
popular culture. Whether for you that meant the DIY riot
grrrls of American punk rock, the Girl Power of British
pop stars the Spice Girls, or the TV action heroine Xena:
Warrior Princess, the pump was definitely primed for a
fierce female to take charge of vampire slaying.

Premiering in spring of 1997 on the WB TV network
in America, the television series *Buffy the Vampire Slayer*
(a reworking of a 1992 film of the same name) introduced a whole new kind of vampire hunter: the blonde
high school cheerleader. In the world of Buffy Summers
(played by Sarah Michelle Gellar), vampires have demon
souls, drawn, along with battalions of other baddies, to
the "Hellmouth" underneath her town of Sunnydale,
California. It's not just her job to protect her friends
and neighbours from the vampires and other monsters,
it's her destiny to keep evil from breaking through from
Hell dimensions and overrunning humanity. Creator Joss

Whedon used vampires to write a story about the struggles of adolescence, where even trivial battles can seem epic. It was hugely successful, spawning seven seasons, a spin-off (*Angel*) and continuing on in comic book form. Dissecting the "Buffyverse" has been become a full-time job for some fans and academics, as its layers of meaning run deep. What's interesting for our discussion is how Buffy is predestined, considering how many cultures have outlined the specific people who are predestined to become vampires after death (see page 38), but few have marked only certain people for slaying them. The myth now has a Chosen saviour.

Buffy is, at first, a reluctant heroine, but over the course of the series she seizes her destiny to the point of self-sacrifice. She patrols the school, the streets and the cemeteries in search of vampires; she uses martial arts training and trusty wooden stakes to "dust" them, usually accompanied by a witty one-liner befitting a character who was originally envisioned as a valley girl. She's crazy talented at giving good the upper hand over evil, and yet, she's got one major flaw for someone who is supposed to kill vampires: she falls in love with them.

Buffy's romances with the show's two bad-boy bloodsuckers Angel (David Boreanaz) and Spike (James Marsters) are tormented ones. Because the lines between the living and the undead are not supposed to be crossed in this way. While Angel and Spike are not particularly good boyfriends, they do love and protect her, and her friends too. So are they still monsters? Should they be destroyed? And what about human/vampire sex? (Yes, it happens.) We've come a long way from Van Helsing and his men fighting to save the chaste Mina Murray from Dracula's evil influences, or the Serbian widow who flees town to escape unsettling bedroom visits from her undead husband. Buffy takes a vampire to prom.

Meanwhile, the vampires of books were becoming increasingly interesting to female readers, who were turning not necessarily to traditional horror, or even Anne Rice, but to the burgeoning genre of vampire chick lit. Usually written by women, these stories did not feature virgins swooning in the presence of creepy undead counts and princes. Instead, like Buffy, the main female characters were all business, and their business was often taking charge of the vampire problem. Yes, by the 1990s, vampire slayer was now a legitimate career choice for young women (at least fictional ones). Canadian fantasy author Tanya Huff's Blood Books series, starting with 1991's *Blood Price*, revolved around detective Vicki Nelson, who investigates supernatural bad guys, and whose partner in crime-fighting is a 450-year-old vampire/romance author. (It was turned into a short-lived television show called *Blood Ties* in 2007.) In 1993, American author Laurell K. Hamilton's novel *Guilty Pleasures* introduced Anita Blake, necromancer and U.S. marshal. In a world where humans and supernaturals coexist, Blake is tasked with slaying vampires who break the law. Like Buffy, she is trained in martial arts. (Although she also carries a handgun.) Like Buffy, she has intimate relations with vampires. (Although these are much more explicit.) Again, we have a heroine slayer whose job conflicts with her feelings, and vampires who can be both good and evil, monstrous and sexy. The Anita Blake: Vampire Hunter series now spans over 20 books, and while it eventually took a turn towards explicit erotica, other writers were concentrating on a different market.

Youth Springs Eternal

"Are you frightened of me now?" —Edward Cullen, *Twilight*

It simply cannot be overstated just how much the Twilight Saga changed vampires. I distinctly remember when American author Stephenie Meyer's first book, *Twilight*, came out in 2005. I reviewed it for a horror magazine, though it was by no means horror fiction, this love affair between ordinary high school girl Bella Swan and undead hunk Edward Cullen. But it was a very good Romeo and Juliet story that happened to have some vampires in it. I believe I called it "breathtaking." There was nothing about Edward that made me believe he could challenge the mighty Dracula, the immortal Lestat—hell, even the brooding Angel—as the poster boy for vampires every-where. I certainly would never have predicted the novel would become one of the most widely read, bestselling books of all time.

And yet here we are, less than a decade later, and *Twilight* is not just popular, it's a phenomenon. The book's sequels—*New Moon* (2006), *Eclipse* (2007) and *Breaking Dawn* (2008)—came fast, followed immediately by the Hollywood feature films, which concluded with a two-part adaptation of *Breaking Dawn* (2011, 2012). The stars of those films, Kristen "Bella" Stewart and Robert "Edward" Pattinson, are about as famous as two young actors can get.

We're talking week-long camp-outs for movie premiere tickets level fandom here. For the "Twihards," vampires = Twilight. A quick glance at the young adult section of your local library and its mountains of *Twilight* rip-offs will reveal the extent to which this series has changed the business of vampire storytelling.

Whether or not you appreciate the masses of screaming teen girl readers crashing the vampire party—and an overwhelming number of horror fans do not—the fact is that Meyer rewrote the rulebook, and didn't just get away with it, she changed vampire mythology on a massive scale. Not only did a legend that has always been not-so-subtly all about sex become a way to talk about abstinence, the way in which Meyer destroys her vampires (or doesn't) is significant too. Consider her approach to sunlight. The most noted physical characteristic of her vampires is that they are gorgeous. Nothing too new there. Oh, and they sparkle. Instead of being weakened or killed by sunlight, exposure to it makes their already flawless skin twinkle and glisten. It's kind of like a full-body halo. But, along with their other supernatural powers—which can include mind-reading and shielding others from harm, in addition to the more common incredible strength and lightning fast speed—it's something they need to keep a secret. (Which is why Edward and his Cullen "family" live in the foggy Pacific Northwest; having to stay hidden in bright daylight hours would make it difficult to attend high school.) So in her own way, Meyer *has* made the sun dangerous for the Twilight vampires, because the first rule of their bite club is that you don't talk about bite club. That's pretty much the only rule actually, and the vampires running things will kill to protect it. So to step out into the sun-light and attract attention from humans with your magical sparkling party trick is a supreme transgression punish-able by death. And not a painless, instant staking either. Meyer kills off her vamps by having them rip each other to pieces—with their bare hands. (Horror fans, if they can get over the whole sparkling thing, might be impressed with the viciousness in which these scenes are depicted in the films.) Sacred objects don't harm them. There are no human slayers with specialized weapons. No, if they don't break the rules or run afoul of their werewolf enemies, these vamps truly are immortal. So as often as they are dismissed as harmless heartthrobs, they are also, in a way, über-vamps. They simply cannot be stopped by humans.

Since then, vampires have been consistently slaying at the box office and on booksellers' lists, dominating mass media and public consciousness like never before. *The Vampire Diaries*, *True Blood*, *Underworld*, *Being Human*, *Abraham Lincoln: Vampire Hunter*, a remake of *Fright Night* and on and on. Not to mention the harder horror crowd hitting back with gory films like *30 Days of Night*, *Daybreakers* and *Let the Right One In*, or the Stephen King–approved comic book series *American Vampire*. Yeah, zombies and werewolves are hot too, but the bloodsuckers—well, they just won't die. That doesn't mean many people, real and imagined, haven't tried to kill them.

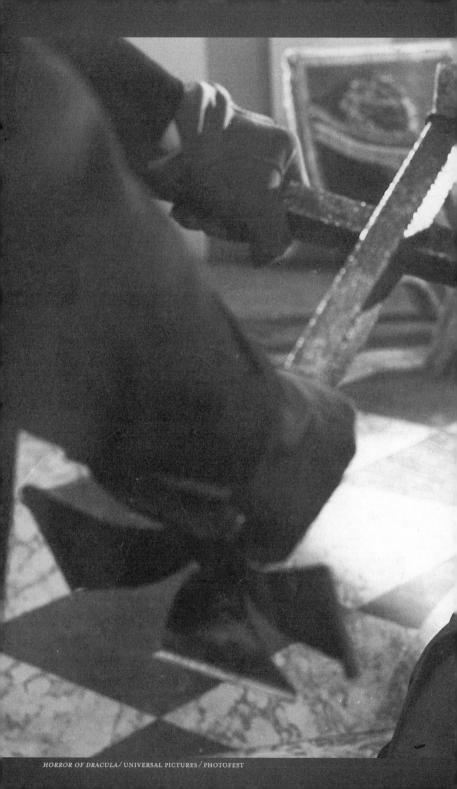

CHAPTER TWO

DETECTION, PREVENTION AND PROTECTION

They say an ounce of prevention is worth a pound of cure. When dealing with vampires, maybe a pound of flesh and a pint of blood too. Before detailing the various tactics said to destroy vampires completely, we should consider some less drastic measures, as well as the ways one can keep a dead person from coming back to life and becoming a nuisance in the first place.

For centuries, superstitions about vampire prevention have circulated across Europe and North America, along with suggested ways to protect oneself—there's quite a bit more to it than simply stocking up on garlic and holy water. You can find an overwhelming amount of this information in hefty studies of European folklore, and the highlights are included in many contemporary documentaries and books about the origins of our vampire obsessions. Few writers have mined this territory for their fictional stories, seemingly content with the handful of tropes so well established by Bram Stoker's *Dracula*, or inventing their own original mythology. But while less known to the modern vampire enthusiast, these historical accounts and legends remain fascinating, often amusing and, yes, sometimes downright frightening.

Detection

"Select a young lad who is a pure maiden. Put him on a young stallion who has not mounted his first mare, coal-black without a speck of white. Ride into a cemetery in and out among the graves and if there is one that the horse refuses to pass, that is where the vampire lies." —Dom Calmet, *Treaty on the Apparitions of Spirits and Vampires*

Sure, you could wait until someone with hungry eyes and a bite mark on their neck shows up in your bedroom looking for a midnight snack. But if you're really keen to find a vampire, you should be a lot more proactive. Various folk traditions claim it's possible to detect a potential vampire long before death, outlining certain conditions that make an individual prone to postmortem reanimation. In Paul Barber's *Vampires, Burial, and Death*, he lists six of these: predisposition, predestination, things that are done to people, things that they do, things that happen to them and things that are left undone. For simplicity, I've divided these into two categories: destiny and deviance.

Vampires are commonly determined at birth. Pity the red-headed child born with teeth, for example. In places such as Greece, Serbia, Bulgaria and Romania, gingers were once seen as suspicious, as occult-obsessed British clergyman Montague Summers wrote in his 1928

English translation of the 1486 witchhunting manual *Malleus Maleficarum*: "Those whose hair is red, of a certain peculiar shade, are unmistakably vampires." Not just any vampires either—some considered them descendants of Judas. Yeah, Judas Iscariot was a vampire and all the red-headed revenants are of his bloodline. (See the section on silver for more thoughts about that.)

Any abnormality at birth could be cause for concern. In Poland, if you were born with teeth, some believed you were destined to become a vampire, which they call either a *ohyn*, *vjeszczi* or *wupji*. According to the Kashubs (an ethnic group from Poland who have settled in, amongst other places, the tiny town of Wilno, Ontario, in Canada), the only remedy against this kind of future vampirism was to extract the teeth from the infants. The Kashubs also feared those born with a red caul, a piece of amniotic membrane that naturally surrounds an unborn baby in the womb. Coming out into the world with some of the caul still stuck on your head is considered good luck in many different cultures around the world. The Kashubs, however, looked suspiciously on newborns bearing a caul red in colour instead of the usual white, considering it a sign that the mother cavorted with demons (it's actually caused by hemorrhages) and a predisposition in the newborn to become a vampire. Luckily, they had a means to reverse the child's fate. As reported in the 1972 study "Vampires, Dwarves and Witches Among the Ontario Kashubs" by Jan Perkowski, "if one takes the [caul] from off the head of a future *vjeszczi*, dries it, grinds it to dust when the child is seven years old, and gives it to the child with his drink, all danger is averted." Perkowski doesn't offer any advice to parents on how to explain to a fussy eater that this is for his or her own good to guard against coming back from the dead.

In Greece, it's not so much how you came into the world, but when. Children born between Christmas and Epiphany (January 6) were considered doomed to become *callicantzaros*, a kind of half-human, half-demon vampire with talons that lives in the underworld and comes back to Earth to tear its family members to pieces during the Christmas holidays. Parents wishing to prevent this fate for their offspring born during Yule could hold their infants' feet over a flame until their toenails were singed off.

Other rumoured potential vampires include the illegitimate children of illegitimately born parents, or the seventh son of a seventh son. So there are plenty of ways you can be born into this fate. But should you manage to have none of these risk factors, that doesn't mean you're free to do as you please in life. Quite the contrary. Unlike in vampire movies, where it's well established that the most common, if not only, way to become a vampire is to be bitten by one and/or to drink its blood, in historical accounts it is usually one's own actions that bring on the curse of undeath.

As Montague Summers points out in *The Vampire, His Kith and Kin*, "The vampire is one who has led a life of more than ordinary immorality and unbridled wickedness. A man of foul, gross and selfish passions, of evil ambitions, delighting in cruelty and blood." If that seems to cover a lot of ground (and many people you know), you're right. According to various experts, the list of people targeted for future vampirism includes: alcoholics, robbers, godless folk, prostitutes, murder victims, arsonists, witches, werewolves (?!), "deceitful and treacherous barmaids" and, as Paul Barber points out, "people who are distinguished primarily by being different from the people who make the lists." Just like witch-hunting, vampire hunting was a way to solve mysterious bad luck by scapegoating the most unpopular folks in town.

Okay, so maybe deviant, anti-social or blasphemous types *are* sometimes worthy of suspicion, but it's still quite a leap from being a drunk to being a bloodsucking murderer. Plus, there were other categories of potential vampires that are clearly not to blame for their actions, such as victims of a stroke or accidental drowning. Barber cites a report documented by Polish theologian Felix Haase of a case in 1506: "we do not dignify with burial the bodies of those who are drowned or murdered . . . instead we drag them into the fields and fence in the place with stakes." Haase goes on to explain how, when the weather was too cold and spring did not bring a good bounty, this community would blame its misfortune not on the weather, but on vampirism. Then they would just figure out which recently buried person had drowned or been murdered, dig up that corpse and throw it somewhere out of the way, unburied. "We believe, in our great foolishness, that his burial is the cause of the cold." Foolish, yes. Alone in worrying about proper burial? No.

Of all the types at risk for vampirism, particular attention was paid to the bodies of suicides or the excommunicated. In Christian societies, these were the worst of behavioural infractions, requiring a penalty so serious it would follow you after death. Suicides were considered the lowest of the low and not deemed worthy of a proper burial in a church graveyard; they would be thrown to the dogs (literally), dumped in a pit on the outskirts or, if buried at all, placed at a crossroads. All because of the fear that a suicide would return after death as a revenant. Excommunication—being banned from the Church for some extremely bad sin—also doomed the body to remain whole after death and its soul in limbo, rather than decomposing naturally while the soul travelled to a spiritual realm. In Greece, in particular, it was said excommunicated bodies didn't decompose until receiving absolution from religious officials. A fear of coming back from the dead was used by the Church as a tool to get people to behave, not unlike threats of going to Hell. Be good kids, or be transformed into a bloodsucker. (You'd be hard pressed to use that against today's Twihards.)

And so, should sudden mysterious deaths start to befall a community, it was to the sinners and cursed that suspicion would turn—and then the wannabe vampire hunters would get to work.

A Vamp By Any Other Name

A field guide to the world of vampires, including vampiric-like spirits and demons, with notes on prevention and protection.

Baobhan-sith	Scotland	A seductive and ferocious female fairy that feasts on the blood of male travellers. Appears often in a green dress and with cloven feet.
Bhuta	India	The evil spirit of someone who died suddenly or violently come back in the form of floating mist to reanimate other corpses.
Blutsauger	Bavaria, southern Germany	Name translates to "bloodsucker." Protect yourself from this ghoulish vamp by getting a black dog and painting an extra set of eyes on it.
Brahmaparush	India	Eats your brain, drinks blood from your skull, rips out your intestines, wraps itself in them, then dances around.
Callicantzaro	Greece	Child revenant that devours its living siblings during Christmastime. Prevention includes singeing toes and feet.
Dearg-due	Ireland	Name translates to "red bloodsucker." Protection involves pilling stones upon its grave.
Dhampir	Balkans	Half-breed child of human mother and vampire father; often makes a good vampire slayer.

Dubbelsüger	Northern Germany	Name translates to "double sucker." A child not properly weaned that after death attacks the breasts of its living relatives.
Eretica	Russia	A heretic in life, rising to haunt the living. Has power of the evil eye.
Katakhana	Crete, Greece	Excommunicated in life, murderous revenant in death for 40 days. To destroy, cut off its head and boil in vinegar.
Krvoijac	Bulgaria	Smoke or drink during Lent? Come back as this vampire. Wild roses planted atop coffin should chain it to the grave.
Kudlak	Slovenia, Croatia	Child born with a caul will come back from the dead. Hunted by its nemesis *kresnik*, local vampire slayer.
Kukuthi	Albania	Also known as a *lugat*; can be destroyed by cutting its hamstrings, or if bitten by a wolf, after which is confined to the grave.
Lampir	Bosnia	Associated with plagues, usually the first to die in a family. Best to exhume and burn the body.
Langsuir	Malaysia	Female who died in childbirth and comes back from the dead for revenge. Has hole in back of its neck through which it drinks blood. Destroy by cutting off hair and stuffing it into the hole.

Liderc Nadaly	Hungary	Power to kill by sex and seduction. Destroyed by nail to the temple.
Moroii	Romania	Name translates to "living vampire"; a kind of sorcerer. Consorts with the *strigoi*.
Motetz Dam	Hebrew	Name translates to "bloodsucker"; your ordinary vamp. Stock a Star of David, not a crucifix.
Muroni	Wallachia, Romania	A shapeshifter. Destroy by staking nail through forehead.
Nachzehrer	Northern Germany, Kashub, Bavaria	Translates to "night waster"; feeds off living family. Destroyed by decapitation, with head separated by wall of dirt and reburied.
Nelapsi	Slovakia	It has the looks that kill. A crushing embrace too. Near impossible to destroy: nail the hair, limbs and clothes to the coffin to keep it down.
Neuntöter	Germany	Translates to "killer of nine," for it takes nine days after death to transform. To prevent this, place a lemon in its mouth at burial.
Nosferatu	Romania	Ah, the classic. Fire a shot into its grave, impale with a stake.
Ohyn	Poland	Born with teeth? Destined to return to eat your family. Preventative measure is to pull the teeth out of infant's mouth.

Penanggalan	Malaysia	Female head and neck with intestines dragging behind who stalks children; place sharp thorns in the home to snare her intestines and trap her 'til dawn.
Pijsvica	Slovenia	The reanimation of an extreme sinner, usually the sin was incest. Hard to kill: try decapitation and place head between legs before reburial.
Sampiro	Albania	Wears high heels. Yup.
Strigoi	Romania	Translates to "dead vampire." Stick nine spindles into the ground to pierce corpse before it can rise from the grave.
Tenatz	Montenegro	Demonically possessed, can shapeshift into a rat. Kill by staking, burning, hamstringing; preferably by a priest.
Ubour	Bulgaria	Prefers animal dung to blood for feeding. Emits luminescent light. Killed by "bottling" by a professional *vampirdzhija*.
Upior	Poland	Has barbed tongue, roams in daylight. Blood found in its coffin is baked into bread and eaten for protection.
Upyr	Russia	Prefers to feed on the blood of children. Holy water and a stake to the chest to dispatch.
Ustrel	Bulgaria	Feeds on cattle; can be killed by a wolf.

Vampyras	Macedonia	Bull-like appearance. Burn exhumed corpses in hot oil and impale long nail through stomach.
Vourdkalak	Russia	A beautiful but evil woman cursed to feed only upon the blood of those she loves.
Vrykolaka	Greece	Scald body in hot oil before staking.
Vudkolak	Serbia	Also refers to werewolves and can be a vampire/werewolf shifter. Place coin in mouth at burial to prevent reanimation.

Prevention

"The partial body and skull of the woman showed her jaw
forced open by a brick—an exorcism technique used on
suspected vampires." —*National Geographic*, March 10, 2009

The handling of dead bodies is a highly ritualized affair,
all around the world, that dates back to the beginning
of humankind. Even in times of peace and prosperity,
proper burial rites are paramount to ensuring a healthy
environment for the living and swift and safe passage for
the dead to whatever afterlife destination a given belief
system prescribes. And in times of war, plague and pesti-
lence, the rules for preparing and disposing of a body are
of great importance indeed, especially if you are worried
about keeping those potential vampires from coming back
to life.

In most of Europe, and in some parts of Asia, traditions recommended that the living stand guard over the
dead body to prevent animals, most often a cat, from
leaping over the corpse before it could be buried; the cat
could transfer its spirit into the body and magically reanimate the deceased. Relatives would keep watch all night
long. Locking up animals during the funeral process was
also considered wise.

For the actual burial, restricting the movements of the
body in the grave was most important to keep a prospective

vampire from clawing its way out of the dirt and wandering around at night. Different societies had different ideas about how best to bind the corpse: in Burma, they tied the toes and thumbs together; in Finland, it was the knees. The 1774 publication *Travels into Dalmatia* by Alberto Fortis reported that Serbians and Croatians practised hamstringing—cutting behind the knees, to hamper walking—and pricked the whole body with pins.

In the days before coffins, bodies were commonly wrapped in a shroud, which could be used against the would-be vampire by placing thorns from, say, a rose bush upon it; should the vampire try to get up, it would become snagged and entangled, unable to rise.

The Chuvash (ethnic Turks currently inhabiting Russia) nailed the corpse to the coffin. Unlike staking, this is not about damaging the body, but was in order to attach it to its resting place, and it could be done through the head, stomach, feet or legs; Wallachians had a similar practice, though they preferred a long nail pierced through the skull. Nailing clothes or hair to the coffin was a less gory option, as was rolling the body in a carpet, as the Bulgarians were said to do.

In some cases, you didn't need to restrict the entire body, just the mouth. Slavs placed thorns under the tongue of a corpse to prevent it from sucking blood. In 2009, an archaeological excavation near Venice, Italy, uncovered a skeleton in a 16th century plague grave with a brick shoved into its mouth; experts believe it's the remains of a suspected "chewing vampire" whose jaw was immobilized at burial. (For the German vampire, *neuntöter*, it was enough to place a lemon in the mouth as an offering against potential evil, indicating that sometimes a symbolic gesture would suffice.) Romanians believed that resuscitating spirits entered the body through the mouth, eyes, ears and nose and would thus sprinkle incense into those orifices. According to 1877's *Excerpts on Bulgarian Vampire Folklore Belief* by S.G.B. St. Clair and Charles A. Brophy, a Bulgarian witch could concoct a potion of excrement (a favourite food of their local vamps) mixed with poisonous herbs to stuff into any holes in the ground above the tomb by which the revenant may escape as mist. You could also dig a grave twice as deep as usual, bury the corpse face down (so if they did wake up they could only claw themselves deeper into the earth) and finally place heavy stones upon the grave, as the Irish did against the potential *dearg-due*.

Modern storytellers have also seized upon the idea of severely restricting a vampire instead of killing them, particularly in times when destruction is impossible. *Dark Shadows* star Barnabas Collins was trapped in his coffin wrapped in chains for a hundred years; Skinner Sweet of the comic *American Vampire* and the Buffyverse's Angel were both imprisoned and dumped underwater. Meanwhile, *The Vampire Diaries* immobilizes vampires by drying them out of blood, as well as with an elaborate "desiccation" spell that has been used against particularly troublesome vamps and hybrids.

Even with all these precautions, a vampire may still rise. So you could plan to keep it from travelling very far by placing large quantities of small things, such as pebbles, or grains of millet or seeds, about the grave, for the vampire would be compelled to stop and count them all. In Bosnia, guests at wakes would put hawthorn twigs in their clothes and then drop them in the street on their way home, so that if the deceased was a vampire thinking of following them, it would become distracted by picking up twigs instead. I guess vampires were early sufferers of OCD. Vampires were equally obsessed with knots and nets. In Germany, they'd bury the corpse with nets to keep it busy untying the knots should it wake up; similarly, Gypsies draped fishnets over the doors of their houses because vampires would have to count all the knots before entering. Even the *chiang-shih* (see sidebar), which is notoriously unstoppable, could be slowed down by scattering rice along its path.

Very few of these superstitions and practices have been kept alive in modern films and fiction. Perhaps this is because they are not nearly as seductive as being bitten by an unnaturally attractive stranger, but it might also be because they are rooted in old-fashioned fears that no longer haunt us, namely the mysteries of disease, contagion and decomposition. However, some ancient vampire folklore has survived to present day, in particular the ways in which the living can guard against the creatures that threaten us in the night, of which there remain plenty.

The Chinese Vampire Chiang-shih

Of all the demons and spirits with vampire-like tendencies haunting the globe, the one that most resembles the European *nosferatu* is the Chinese *chiang-shih*. This nocturnal revenant has red eyes, fangs, long talon-like nails and a ghoulish white or green face. As with the West's vampire, *chiang-shih* are believed to result from a bad death (suicide, violence) or improper burial. But it also has a culturally specific origin:

the Chinese concept that we have two souls, a superior rational soul and an inferior irrational soul called *p'ai*. The *p'ai* lingers in the body after death until a person is properly decomposed, and it's this restless soul that can reanimate the corpse and haunt the living, absorbing their life essence or just plain ripping off their heads. The *chiang-shih* is usually seen hopping, arms outstretched, as if still suffering from rigor mortis.

As with any good monster legend, this one has complicated protection and destruction instructions. Like the Western vampire, the *chiang-shih* hates garlic and mirrors; it will run from its own reflection. They are not fond of salt or loud noises, like thunder, either. If you place rice around their coffins, that should keep them from rising. Or use a broom to literally sweep them back in. If one does get out and go on the attack, it can be put to sleep if a piece of yellow paper with a spell written on it is stuck to its forehead. You can also hurt it with a thread stained with black ink (instant garrotte!) or if all else fails hold your breath and hope that it passes by you, unawares. Sadly, these are just delay tactics, as the *chiang-shih* is virtually indestructable. Ultimately, the only way to destroy it is with a whole lot of fire.

These characteristics come partly from folklore and partly from horror cinema. Do yourself a favour and skip the mind-bogglingly lame Hammer/Hong Kong mash-up *Legend of the 7 Golden Vampires* (1974) and instead seek out *Mr. Vampire*, a seriously fun horror/comedy flick from 1985, full of martial arts action, ghosts and gags that kids especially will love. *Mr. Vampire* launched four sequels, a TV show and a wave of other "hopping vampire" films and TV series with such silly names as *Robo Vampire* (1988), *Dragon Against Vampire* (1985), and *My Date with a Vampire* (1998). Since then, the *chiang-shih* has taken its rightful place on the world stage of monsters, even making an appearance in Kim Newman's seminal historical horror novel *Anno Dracula* (1992) — working for Fu Manchu, of course.

Protection

Have you ever knocked on wood after making a joke about death or to prevent bad luck? Then you have bought into the concept of an apotropaic: a kind of magic charm or spell to ward off evil. There are several well-known apotropaics which can be employed to protect the living from a vampire's supernatural powers, to restrict and repel them, and potentially even cause the undead grievous bodily harm. Popularized in books and movies, they have their origins in traditional folk remedies and rituals.

GARLIC

"Shortly after I had arrived, a big parcel from abroad came for the Professor. He opened it . . . and showed a great bundle of white flowers . . . 'These is for you, Miss Lucy. . . . This is medicinal but you do not know how. I put him in your window, I make pretty wreath, and hang him around your neck so that you sleep well.' . . . Lucy had been examining these flowers. Now she threw them down saying . . . 'Why, these flowers are only common garlic.'" —Dr. Seward's diary, *Dracula*

Dearest Lucy, there is nothing common about garlic. A bulb plant of the allium family (which also includes onions and leeks), it has long been valued for its healing properties, a kind of "universal remedy" for everything from insect bites and colds to worms and even leprosy (!) dating back to ancient Egypt. Also, vampires hate it.

How we know this is tricky to unravel. Bram Stoker famously included garlic in *Dracula* as a means to keep a vampire from entering your home, which scholars say he discovered in his research into legends of vampires in Transylvania. But the text he's known to have consulted, Emily Gerard's *Transylvanian Superstitions* (1885), contains nothing about garlic's ability to ward off an attack, only that Romanians sometimes place garlic in the mouth of an exhumed vampire. However, by 1926, folklorist Agnes Murgoci published in *The Vampire in Roumania* that "it is known that a man is a vampire if he does not eat garlic; this idea is also found among the South Slavs." Particularly on St. Andrew's Eve, St. George's Eve and before Easter and the New Year, she wrote, "Windows should be anointed with garlic in the form of a cross, garlic put on the door and everything in the house, and all the cows in the cow shed should be rubbed with garlic. When vampires do enter, they do by the chimney or the keyhole, so these orifices require special attention when garlic is rubbed in. Even though the window is anointed with garlic, it is wisest to keep it shut."

This description mirrors the actions of Professor Van Helsing in Stoker's novel—he uses garlic to protect Lucy from further visits by Dracula—but neither Stoker nor Murgoci offer an explanation of why this should work. What legitimate reason could vampires have for avoiding garlic? We know it smells strong, so maybe they just really, really hate garlic breath? As University of Albany chemistry professor Eric Block notes in his definitive book

Garlic and Other Alliums: The Lore and the Science (2010), the pungent aroma is detectable even with extensive dilution, so presumably anyone/thing with superior olfactory senses would be extra sensitive to it. This may account for the legend that garlic wards off snakes, which have heightened smell through their tongues. In *Vampire Forensics* (2010), historian Mark Collins Jenkins notes that people infected with rabies are hypersensitive to strong smells and, citing a correlation between reports of rabies outbreaks and vampire epidemics in Hungary in early 1700s, suggests villagers may have been mistaking garlic-avoiding rabies victims for vampires. Folks have been known to use other gross-smelling objects to keep away potential evil, such as rotting food, feces and burned animal parts. Surely, when compared to those options, garlic, which is widely available and also keeps longer, would be your go-to choice.

The smell of garlic alone would merely annoy a vamp, rather than harm them, but contact with the stuff can be painful—even for humans. Raw garlic, particularly when sliced or crushed (which releases the compound allicin), is a potent irritant that can rapidly penetrate our skin and cause burns and blistering lesions. Block notes that sliced raw garlic on the tongue and lips elicits a painful burning sensation in the skin, cornea and mucosa. There are also drawbacks to ingesting or inhaling garlic or a juice made from garlic, which is sometimes prescribed as a remedy to promote digestion but in excess is "apt to produce headache, thirst, febrile heat and inflammatory diseases and sometimes discharges blood from hemorrhoidal vessels," according to Block. Too much ingested raw garlic has proved fatal to children. In Matheson's *I Am Legend*, the last human on Earth, Robert Neville, conducts a scientific investigation on garlic's compounds to figure out how and why it works against the vampire hordes at his door; he determines that it's the allyl sulphide in its oil that vampires hate and that the smell of garlic is an allergen to anyone infected with vampire bacteria. But since vampires can withstand so much trauma to their bodies, surely they'd be much less susceptible to any of these dangers than we are? Unless the answer is not scientific, but supernatural.

For all of its healing properties, some cultures consider garlic the stuff of evil, impure. Muslim legend has it that when Satan exited the Garden of Eden, garlic sprang up where his left foot had been. The Bower Manuscript, a fifth century Buddhist medical treatise, claims garlic originated from the blood of a demon. In modern India, garlic is considered inappropriate for offering to the Hindu gods. One might think all this would inspire vampires to embrace garlic, not reject it, but there are an equal number of cultures that believe garlic can be wielded against malevolent spirits. In Greece, garlic is still considered a powerful force of protection against spirit possession and the evil eye. Some Malaysians and Chinese parents rub a child's forehead with garlic to protect against vamps; in the Philippines, it's the armpit. But it's those vampire-fearing Slavs, whose traditions involve hanging whole strands of garlic on doors and windows and around their necks, who have had the most influence on the way we perceive the relationship between garlic and vampires, thanks to the popularization of their practices in books and movies.

Ever since Professor Van Helsing brought garlic to Lucy's bedroom in Dracula, almost every vampire story has mentioned the plant, either as a means of protection or, increasingly, to laugh off the idea as outdated superstitious nonsense. The vampire pandemic survival film *Stake Land* (2010) features a garlic scene between the slayer known only as Mister and the orphaned teenager Martin that is serious yet played for laughs. Schooling the boy in the art of vampire killing, Mister teaches Martin to rub garlic oil on his stakes. "Does that work?" asks Martin. Mister: "Can't hurt." Garlic is also a common punchline in vampire-themed humour. In the animated opening sequence for Roman Polanski's 1967 comedy/horror *The Fearless Vampire Killers*, a vamp is scared off by garlic breath.

And so, after decades as a known vampire repellent, garlic is falling out of favour with modern storytellers. Buffy Summers may have been the last of the on-screen slayers to pack it in her vampire killing kit (even if she rarely used it), for all the blockbuster series that have come since—the Twilight Saga, *True Blood*, *The Vampire Diaries*—have made a point of explaining that it doesn't work against their vamps. *True Blood*'s lead vampire Bill Compton declared it "an annoyance, nothing more."

Vervain, the New Garlic?

Garlic isn't the only plant known to be used against vampires. Vervain, a flowering plant also known as verbena, was written into the mythology by *The Vampire Diaries* author L.J. Smith. In her young adult books and the hit television show based upon them, vervain is harmful to vampires and can be used by humans as protection from their mind control.

The reasons for this are as old as *TVD*'s vamps themselves. In the TV series, a witch named Esther created vampires by means of a spell to protect her children and husband with eternal life. In order to restore the balance, Nature created weaknesses in the vampires, among them exposure to vervain. Contact with the plant burns vampire skin, and when ingested it weakens a vampire. Drinking from someone who had been ingesting vervain is equally dangerous. The vampire hunter Alaric Saltzman creates weapons for effective delivery of the plant: vervain darts and vervain grenades. Meanwhile, clever vampires respond to the threat by voluntarily ingesting vervain in small doses in order to develop immunity. One admits drinking it every day for more than a century. As quipped the star vamp Damon Salvatore, "It's an acquired taste."

The other chief characteristic of the plant is that it can protect the living against vampire bewitchment. Humans can add the oil from vervain to a bath or rub it on the skin; dried vervain leaves can be worn in a pouch or jewellery, drunk in tea or placed under your pillow. Unlike lore surrounding garlic, this will not keep vampires from coming near you, but it will prevent them from compelling you to do stupid things or to forget an encounter.

Since the premiere of the TV show in 2009, fans have rushed to figure out if the vervain mythology is true. While it is true that vervain has been used in folk medicine over the years to cure everything from fever to worms, there are no reports of it in old vampire folkore. But given the popularity of *The Vampire Diaries*, don't be surprised if it shows up in the vampire stories of the future.

CRUCIFIXES, HOLY WATER AND OTHER SACRED OBJECTS

Vampire: "Ha ha! Garlic don't work, boys!"
Edgar Frog: "Try the holy water, death breath!"
—*The Lost Boys*

Traditionally, vampires fear religious symbols. The sacred objects most commonly used for protection are Christian: water blessed by a priest, the cross or crucifix and the holy Eucharist or "Host,"—a consecrated unleavened bread or wafer meant to represent the body of Jesus Christ. These are key items in any vampire killing kit and have been used to great effect by many a fictional slayer, sometimes to kill but mostly to repel or maim.

In Stoker's *Dracula*, the crucifix plays a significant role in helping the characters evade vampire attacks. Early in the story, a superstitious gypsy forces a rosary on businessman Jonathan Harker for protection after hearing he is en route to visit Count Dracula at the dreaded Castle Dracula; later, the Count is, in fact, repelled by the sight of it. Professor Van Helsing includes the crucifix in his list of things that vampires hate, claiming it will weaken any powers they may possess, and he wields one several times throughout the novel. There's no evidence that Stoker got the idea to use the crucifix to ward off his vampires from folklore. Rather, it seems he invented the plot device from the not-then-uncommon concepts that vampires are agents of Satan and that the crucifix has sacred powers.

In the Hammer adaptation *Horror of Dracula*, Van Helsing spells out in his journal that the crucifix represents the "power of good over evil." In the film, the professor uses an oversized silver cross from a rosary to repel the vampire Lucy; when pressed against her forehead, it burns her like acid, and she flees. (This has become a prominent use of the crucifix in movies.) He then gives it to the child Tania for protection, and later places one in Dracula's coffin to prevent him from returning to rest there. In the final confrontation with Dracula, Van Helsing, finding himself in a showdown without any weapons, grabs two nearby candelabras and holds them up in the shape of a cross, which repels the Count. This scene created a visual trope since adopted by many other cinematic slayers: since then, we have seen characters use whatever is at hand from baseball bats to tongue depressors—even two of their own fingers—to form an impromptu cross. Van Helsing points out that the crucifix can also be an investigative tool used to reveal someone who is a vampire, or was recently bitten by one. In the Italian horror classic *Black Sunday* (1960), the vampire-witch Asa attempts to fool a doctor into slaying the maiden Katia (whom she resembles) by claiming she is a vampire, but when he notices a crucifix resting safely around Katia's neck, he realizes there is some mistaken identity afoot and stops short of staking the wrong woman.

Bram Stoker's *Dracula* also made good use of the Eucharist wafer, which was more likely to have been used in real life against vampires. As Montague Summers describes in *The Vampire, His Kith and Kin*, wafers have been found in the tombs of saints such as St. Basil, St. Othman and St. Cuthbert, and even modern-day Greeks were known to place one between the lips of the dead at burial, as protection against vampirism. In *Dracula*, Professor Van Helsing imports host wafers from his parish in Amsterdam to London in preparation to fight off the vampires; he uses them first to make a putty to seal up Lucy's tomb "so that the undead may not enter," then later places them in a protection circle around Mina to thwart Dracula's hypnotic advances. (A scene dramatized to great effect in Francis Ford Coppola's 1992 film *Bram Stoker's Dracula*.) Despite all this, the sacred wafer defence never really caught on in popular culture as much as the cross or crucifix, probably because that's a much more dramatic and recognizable prop. Plus, the Eucharist was in many ways replaced by the use of another Christian sacramental: holy water.

The use of holy water against vampires was not nearly as common in folklore as the crucifix or sacred Host. However, it has been eagerly adopted by film and fiction writers, who use it not so much to protect the living but to harm the undead. Like garlic, it's generally something that burns vampire skin like acid (Asher, a master vampire in the Anita Blake: Vampire Hunter novels, is severely scarred on one half of his body and face from being tortured with it) or it acts as poison if ingested (in the *Buffy* episode "Helpless," Buffy tricks a vampire into washing down his prescription pills with a glass of holy water). One of the more creative applications of it was in the movie adaptation of Stephen King's *'Salem's Lot* (1979), where vials of holy water are used as a detection device, their glow indicating the presence of vampires. The good thing about holy water is that it's easily available. Simply visit your local church and steal some (as seen in *The Lost Boys*) or have whatever priest or other man/woman of God you've written into your fictional team bless any water on hand.

Presto. (See 1996's *From Dusk till Dawn*.) On the negative side, it might only work if you actually believe in it.

What if the vampire isn't Christian? *The Fearless Vampire Killers* saw a Jewish vamp laugh off an attempt to repel him with a crucifix: "You've got the wrong vampire!" But increasingly, holy objects from other faiths are being employed. The BBC Television series *Being Human* (which premiered in 2008 in England and was adapted for North America in 2011) has rules around the Star of David. The Jewish symbol can repel a vampire attack, although with the caveats that the bearer must not feel any affection for the vampire or be outnumbered by them, else its effectiveness is diminished; the oldest vampires are also immune to religious relics. And in the young adult urban fantasy book series The Mortal Instruments by Cassandra Clare, vampires are vulnerable to religious symbols from whatever faith they were as humans.

The element of faith is key to the effectiveness of sacred objects against vampires. This is not something we generally see for other tactics—decapitation will do the job whether you believe it will or not. Anne Rice, a Christian herself, created a world where religious icons have no power. In the beginning of *Interview with the Vampire*, Louis calls the "rumour" that his kind cannot look upon a cross "sheer nonsense." While other authors have continued to embrace and expand upon the use of the sacred against vampires (one creative recent story is "The Greatest Trick" by Steve Vernon, in which a man repels "Jedi-Lugosi mind control tricks" by wearing a set of contact lenses blessed by three holy men), the influence of Rice and her bestselling Vampire Chronicles series has loomed large over supernatural storytelling for decades, with Christian icons appearing less and less often, a reflection of the ever-diminishing influence of religion in modern mythmaking.

Mirror, Mirror on the Wall, Who Is the Most Undead of All?

We've seen how, in historical vampire accounts, ways to detect a vampire range from abnormal births to deviant lifestyles to suspiciously fresh corpses. There's not much talk about how to distinguish a living vampire from a human. That's because in folklore, the vampire is usually already known in the community. The fictional vampire, however, is most often a stranger, surreptitiously seducing the local women who can't seem to tell the difference between a real man and the walking dead. (Not sure what that tells you about the local men.)

Bram Stoker imagined one way for his characters to figure out something was not quite right about Count Dracula: he would not appear in mirrors. In an early scene in Dracula's castle, the visiting Jonathan Harker is shaving when the Count touches him from behind. "It amazed me that I had not seen him," Harker writes in his diary, "since the reflection of the glass covered the whole room behind me . . . there was no reflection of him in the mirror!" The Count actually grabs the "wretched thing" and flings it out of the castle window, shattering the glass on the stones below.

The idea was purely a literary invention, and is right there in Stoker's handwritten research notes for the novel. "No looking glasses in Count's house" and "never can see him reflected in one" top his rules of vampirism. Speculation on his inspiration for this is widespread, and often points to the notion that mirrors reflect the soul (which a vampire doesn't have) or to a theory that we can't see vampires in mirrors because we don't believe in the monsters (a rather Christian point of view). Mirrors have their own set of superstitions, including (of course) that breaking one is bad luck and that one should turn mirrors to the wall when a dead person is in the home (Bulgaria), and to avoid the reflection of a new moon in a mirror (England).

In destroying Harker's shaving mirror, Count Dracula reveals that he knows about this trick, and seeks to avoid being seen not being seen. In the stage play and film versions of *Dracula*, the confrontation is between the Count and Van Helsing, and it firmly established the rule in vampire lore. Until Anne Rice came around in the 1970s with her *Interview with the Vampire*: her vampires Louis and Lestat enjoy looking at their transformed selves; in fact, in one memorable scene the child vamp Claudia throws a fit at her own reflection as she watches her hair grow back after she cut it off. From then on, it's been a hit and miss technique. In *Buffy the Vampire Slayer*'s world, vamps are not seen in mirrors but in *The Vampire Diaries* and *True Blood* they are: Bill Compton actually claims the vampires made up the mirror myth themselves, so they could prove they *weren't* a vampire by appearing in one. And since Bill is older than Bram—his transformation to vampire happening in 1865, a full 25 years before Stoker began writing *Dracula*—maybe he's right.

Rituals

Stefan Salvatore: "What are you doing here?"
Damon Salvatore: "Waiting for Elena to invite me in."
—"Friday Night Bites," *The Vampire Diaries*

Several regional practices to protect people against vampires have also been recorded throughout history. These techniques, more specialized and sometimes rather unusual, have rarely been mentioned in books or films but have survived through folkloric accounts.

The pagan tradition of need-fire has been applied to vampires in Slovakia and Bulgaria. This purification bonfire was used throughout Europe in times of plague or mass cattle sickness to purge suspected evil influences from the area. Specifics as to how to start the fire or who should do it vary, although it usually required extinguishing other fires in the village, lighting two new ones and then driving the cattle between the roaring flames. Smoke from the need-fire was said to drive away vampires.

"Blood bread" is consumed for immunity against vampires in Poland and Russia, as reported by French Benedictine monk and theologian Augustin Calmet in his bestselling 1746 vampire treatise (an English translation was published under the title *The Phantom World* in 1850). First you need to open a vampire's grave and, should you find the corpse swimming in fresh blood, take a sample, mix it with flour and bake it into bread. Oh, and eat it. (The practice was referenced in a vampire-themed episode of *The X-Files*, "3.") Similarly, German ethnologist Ernst Bargheer reported that in Pomerania (in present-day Germany and Poland), you could dip part of the vampire's shroud in its blood, leach the blood out into brandy and drink the mixture for protection. In Hungary, the blood was simply smeared on one's body; it was dirt from the grave you should snack on. In the famous tale of Arnold Paole, the Serbian who believed he'd been infected by a vampire, he claimed he tried this remedy to ward off a transformation, but it obviously didn't work because after his (accidental) death in 1725 neighbours complained he was visiting them in the night. Wallachians didn't need vampire blood, just the lard of a pig slaughtered on St. Ignatius Day be rubbed on "certain parts" (?!) of the body.

One Greek practice has made its way into popular culture, albeit indirectly. According to a 1645 study by Greek theologian and doctor Leo Allatius, it was said that at night vampires wander the villages knocking on doors and calling out victims by name. If you answered, in two days you would die. But the vampire would never call a name twice, so you could thwart their attack by simply not replying until the person at the door says your name twice, a superstition that remains alive in some parts of the country today. It's my view that this is connected to the now common idea that a vampire must be invited inside in order to enter a home, the origins of which are undocumented.

The invitation rule has become one of the key ways to protect oneself against a vampire attack in modern times. They can't bite you if they can't touch you, and they can't touch you if you stay inside your own home and refuse to let them in. Should they try to enter anyway, sometimes they encounter a kind of forcefield or, once inside, experience great pain. In the 2004 Swedish novel *Let the Right One In* by John Ajvide Lindqvist, the child vampire Eli explains to her boy companion, Oskar, that she cannot cross his apartment door without an invite. "What happens if I don't?" he teases. Eli enters, seemingly without effort or consequences—at least at first. Within moments, tears of blood appear in her eyes, her face flushed red. Lindqvist writes how Eli's lips "twisted in pain" while her eyes looked like they had "sunk into their sockets." She starts to bleed from every orifice (that we can see) and all the pores of her body. In horror, Oskar shouts out that she is welcome to come in, at which point Eli relaxes, gradually returning to "normal." The scene was played out dramatically in the 2008 Swedish film adaptation, and its 2010 U.S. remake, *Let Me In*.

Over the years, different storytellers have added their own twists to this basic rule, but at this point most conceivable scenarios have been covered. It is well established that vampires can only be kept out of homes owned and/ or occupied by humans. So, if you're in another vampire's dwelling, any vampire can waltz right in. Hotels and other public places remain grey areas, but usually in favour of the vampires. In the *Buffy the Vampire Slayer* movie, a gang of vamps descends on the high school dance; Buffy thinks she and her friends are safe because she hasn't invited them in until it's pointed out that, since they were senior students in life, they had already been invited. Oops. Vampires have the upper hand in *True Blood* as well: they have been known to hypnotize (or "glamour") a human into saying "yes, come in" when they really mean "over my dead body."

One trick humans can play: revoking your invitation. In *'Salem's Lot*, the vampire Mike enters the home of his friend Matt, who had invited him in before either of them knew he was undead. When Mike begins to attack, Matt uses a crucifix to distract Mike long enough to shout, "Get out of here! I revoke my invitation!" The vampire screams "a high undulating sound full of hate and pain," then steps backwards towards a window and falls away into the dark of night.

But don't get too smug: a vampire can just destroy your house. In the 2011 remake of *Fright Night*, young horror movie fan turned slayer Charlie Brewster (Anton Yechin) takes shelter in his home but his neighbourhood baddie Jerry Dandrige (Colin Farrell) simply rips the gaslines from the place and lights it on fire, quipping, "Don't need an invitation if there's no house."

By now, you may have noted that many ways of preventing a vampire attack, or the transformation into a vampire, are similar to those commonly believed to destroy an existing vampire, although there are important distinctions if you're looking to inflict a fatal blow. It is to that which we now turn our attention.

Greece's Vampire Island

In the world of vampire tourism, Romania gets all the glory—and all the gift shop revenue. A visit to Castle Dracula in Transylvania is on many a wish list. But what about Greece? This country's vampire lore goes back just as far as the tales from eastern Europe. It even boasts a "vampire island," allegedly the most vampire-infested location in the world.

In Greece, vampires are more commonly known by the name *vrykolakas*. The myth comes from a longstanding belief that improper burial rites will curse a body to remain trapped in the ground forever, unable to pass on to the afterlife. With Slavic immigration to Greece came the idea of the revenant, the vampire, although the *vrykolakas* is less violent than the typical bloodsucker, more concerned with playing tricks on the living, such as "overturning furniture, extinguishing the lamps." (Also, getting together to eat green beans in the fields. The original vegetarian vamps?) The Greek Orthodox church got into the game, preaching that excommunication would doom one to vampirism. And soon enough, *vrykolakas* panics began.

Around the turn of the 18th century, visiting scholars began documenting accounts of the Greek *vrykolakas*. French botanist Joseph Pitton de Tournefort wrote in his *Relation d'un Voyage du Levant* (1711) of witnessing an actual vampire slaying on the island of Mykonos in 1701. A dead peasant, a victim of murder, was seen walking in the streets around town after his burial. Either by a priest or a butcher (it's unclear), the man's grave was opened, its corpse exhumed and its heart ripped out—causing a great stench they covered by burning incense. (Villagers "infatuated with the idea of the return of the dead" then told of the clouds of smoke that emerged from the corpse.) He described how "one indignity after another" was done to the corpse, from various swords and scimitars shoved into the grave, to covering the dead body in tar, putting it up on a pyre and setting it ablaze. The vampire attacks, and related mania, abated. Well, there at least. Modern archeological excavations on the island of Lesbos have uncovered graves of men buried with spikes through their necks, groins and ankles.

If you couldn't manage to dispatch your vampire yourself, you could send them off to Santorini, the so-called vampire island. This beautiful tourist resort in the Aegean Sea boasts dry, volcanic soil, which prevents the quick decomposition of a corpse. And back when digging up a body was *de rigueur*, a great many were remarkably well preserved, i.e., showing signs of vampirism. Thus, locals became experts on the phenomenon and so other Greeks would ship off their troublesome *vrykolakas* to Santorini. (Rumours about vampires being unable to cross bodies of running water made this trade even more attractive.) Overflow could be rowed across to the neighbouring islands of Thirassia and Kameni, now considered vampire graveyards by some. If you're visiting Santorini, you can hire a boat to take you over: watch for sailors making the sign of the cross with their ropes before tying up to the shore, a sign that superstition persists today. Surprisingly, only one film of note has tapped into the *vrykolakas* legend. The 1945 horror film *Isle of the Dead*, starring Boris Karloff, involves a group of people held captive on a small Greek island during the First Balkan War of 1912. A quarantine is in effect due to a suspected plague ("No one can leave the island!"), which is rather inconvenient when folks start to die off and one young woman is accused of being a *vrykolakas*. So, you know, before booking that summer getaway to Santorini, beware there's a risk you might never come back.

CHAPTER THREE

THE WEAPONS

I. STAKING

"A moment's courage, and it is done."
—Professor Van Helsing, *Dracula*

The most popular way to destroy a vampire is, perhaps not surprisingly, also the oldest: a sharpened wooden stake, driven fearlessly into the heart. It's an iconic image, the climax of many a scary tale, with its origins in the earliest folklore of the bloodsucking revenant. It's also no wonder staking is the go-to tactic, for it's nothing if not practical. A stake is inexpensive and easy to acquire. Officially, it's just a wooden pole, sharpened at the end, the kind usually driven into the ground to mark a spot, hold a sign . . . or torture a witch by tying him/her to it and then lighting a fire. But a fence post, a chair leg, a fallen tree branch, a pencil, pretty much any scrap wood can be used against a vamp in a pinch. Add a hammer or mallet and you have an easy to use, lethal weapon—one that also casts a wonderfully dramatic shadow when held aloft as you creep through a graveyard, crypt or castle basement in search of your prey.

We've seen how superstitions about vampires usually revolved around a dead body rising from its grave and causing harm to loved ones or general mischief in the village, and that what the living wanted was to prevent the dead from getting up and moving around. Fixing the corpse to the grave with a stake proved a simple and effective solution.

Although we've come to associate stakes with attacking the heart, this was not originally the exclusive target; staking a vampire to the ground through any part of the torso would do. The stomach was one particularly popular choice, and definitely easier to access than navigating around the bones of the ribcage that protect the heart. In some regions of Russia, it was common to stake through the mouth, to prevent the vampire from biting or sucking. Yet it was the stake to the heart that captured the imaginations of fiction writers, and has thus stuck with us. Perhaps it was the influence of reports from Romania, where it was believed one type of vampire, the *strigoi*, had two hearts, the second of which keeps the dead alive. Thus, piercing or removing this heart would put an end to the vampire's terror and give peace to the deceased's soul.

As mentioned earlier, if a person was considered likely to return as a vampire after death (due to specific circumstances of birth or anti-social life choices), the staking would happen at the time of burial, as a precaution. But anyone whose family members started dying of mysterious causes after their death could have their grave dug up and, should the signs of vampirism (such as blood in the mouth, "new" fingernails, etc.) be present, have a stake driven through their rotting corpse. This could happen days, weeks or months after death, and it was often the duty of some official from the government or the Church, although there were also professional vampire hunters you could call in. (See chapter four for more on that.) Whether amateur or pro, before springing into action it was a good idea to try to keep from being splashed with vampire blood (which could turn the splashee into a vamp); placing a dried animal hide over the corpse before driving the stake in should take care of it.

Participants in these vampire stakings truly did believe they were destroying a dangerous predator, even if to contemporary, rational eyes all they were really doing was desecrating a dead body in a rather gruesome public ritual. While disinterment and/or defilement of suspected vampires went on unchecked for centuries in the olde countries, eventually the practice fell out of favour with the authorities, who stepped in to enact laws preventing the mutilation of corpses. In 1823 in England, there was an amendment to the law relating to "the Interment of the Remains of any Person found *felo de se*"—suicides. Yes, staking suicides to check for vampirism had become so rampant, the government had to make it illegal. From then on, coroners had to ensure burials of suicides would happen "without any stake being driven through the body of such person." However, not all superstitions were banished: the burial did have to take place in the dark, between nine p.m. and midnight. Because that's not unnerving, not at all.

As Paul Barber notes in *Vampires, Burial, and Death*, staking has two aspects: mechanical and magical. Clearly, a foreign object piercing the internal organs, especially the heart, would kill any living person, and thus is a reasonable thing to try against the undead too. But of all the objects one could use to do this deed—iron rod, knife, sword, pitchfork, etc.—it's the wooden stake which became the standard. Perhaps because of the handiness described above. But it has also continued to be the preferred tool of storytellers, even after the invention of more exciting modern weaponry. Thus, we must acknowledge the magical aspects of staking have helped to secure its place in our imaginations.

In folklore, the wooden stake is often required to be made from a specific type of wood in order to be effective against a vampire. Different cultures have their own rules about this, often related to a tree's particular magical properties in mythology, or perhaps simply because it was regionally available. (You don't see many northern European vampire stories requiring a palm tree, for example.)

Ash is a wood that is strong and flexible. In Norse mythology, an ash tree called the Yggdrasil is responsible for creating the world, including the first man. Ash has often been associated with healing and protection. In England, newborn babies were sometimes given a teaspoon of ash sap to protect against disease, and ash berries were placed in a child's bed to keep malevolent fairies at bay. Apparently, ash could also be used to cure skin problems such as warts. In some European cultures, snakes were said to be repelled by ash leaves, or by a circle drawn with a branch of the tree.

Using ash stakes against vampires was particularly popular in Russia. One such account (taken from the 1897 publication *Aberglaube und Strafecht* by August Löwenstimm) involves a peasant girl named Justina Yuschkov who died in childbirth in 1848, during a time of cholera. A superstitious medical officer blamed the cholera epidemic on a "dissolute girl" who died pregnant, and against the will of the local priest, villagers disinterred Justina's body to check if that might be her. They cut her open ("a bestial operation," wrote the priest) but found no unborn child in her belly, only the dead body of her baby buried with her in the coffin. However, they decided her mouth being open was proof enough of vampirism. As reported, "they drove an ashwood stake through the corpse and reburied her."

More than a century later, author Robert R. McCammon specified the use of ash wood stakes ("two feet long") in his epic novel *They Thirst*, about vampires taking over Los Angeles. His protagonist, police officer Andy Palatizin, is a native of Hungary whose father was turned into a vampire and whose mother became obsessed with tracking their spread across America, so he knows a few things. In The Vampire Diaries series of novels by L.J. Smith published in the 1990s, a stake made from white ash wood is what you need to kill an "Old One," one of the original vampires.

Oak is one of the strongest hardwoods, used for building furniture or even ships. Some of the oldest trees on Earth are oak, and it has become a symbol of strength and endurance. In ancient mythology, oak was associated with thunder. Some published reports of historical vampire accounts specify oak stakes. Löwenstimm's book details the case of suspected witch Marina Kusjmin of the remote Russian community of Tashtamakowa (now Tashtamak), whose corpse was staked with oak wood to try to end a mysterious disease epidemic in 1893. But the most intriguing connection between oak and vampires comes from contemporary TV.

On *The Vampire Diaries*, which debuted in 2009, the white oak is embued with magical properties, thanks to its part in the creation of the original vampires, and a stake formed from its wood is the only way to properly kill one. When these "Originals" discover this, they burn the tree to the ground. Except—surprise!—witches have collected some of the ashes and now use that against them. It's a bit complicated though. A dagger dipped in the white oak ash will kinda, sorta, kill an Original vamp—*if* it's wielded by a human or another Original and not just an ordinary vampire and *if* it's staked in the heart and then left there. Might be easier to locate the one remaining stake made from wood of the white oak, which can bring true death to the otherwise super-hard-to-slay Originals, and destroy every vampire in their bloodline, making it one of the most powerful and devastating weapons ever wielded against a vamp.

Aspen is a strong, soft wood that is difficult to burn. Its notoriety goes back to biblical times: Christ's cross was said to be made from aspen, and legend has it that Judas hanged himself on an aspen tree. The leaves have been used to treat burns and other physical ailments and famed British botanist Dr. Edward Bach prescribed extracts of aspen from his flower remedies to treat fears and terrors "for which there can be given no explanation." It has a long tradition of being used to drive away evil spirits. The Greek word for aspen is *aspis*, which means "shield," and, indeed, some Celts thought shields made from aspen wood had magical properties. Aspen is mentioned in many key reference books about vampire folklore, such as Summers' *The Vampire, His Kith and Kin* and *In Search of Dracula*

(1994) by Raymond T. McNally and Radu R. Florescu, although specific cases are not detailed.

Juniper is an evergreen tree most often used for its aromatic smoke. Burning wood of the juniper has been part of purification rituals or fumigation during times of plague or illness. Muslim Gypsies kept juniper in the house to protect from vampires, or used the wood as a stake, which they thrust into the grave without having to dig up the person. In the supernatural roomies television series *Being Human*, juniper is poison for vampires, causing short-lasting paralysis. One of my favourite juniper stories comes from an article from 2003 in the wacky supermarket tabloid *Weekly World News* called "How to Protect Your Family from the Undead." Check out this tip: "For emergency protection against vampires, drink gin. They're allergic to juniper berries and one sip of gin-laced blood could kill them. Centuries of avoiding juniper has made them highly sensitive to the scent of gin, and if you've drunk it they'll pass you up for a safer and more tasty treat." (To put that in context, the same issue claimed Saddam Hussein was using dinosaurs as weapons for mass destruction!)

Hawthorn is hard and resistant to rot, therefore good for fence posts, which may explain why it's such a popular wood to use against vampires, since those are pretty ready-made stakes. Again, in the Christian bible, some say Christ's crown of thorns was made from hawthorn. In Gaelic folklore, hawthorn marks the entrance to the underworld and is strongly associated with fairy magic. Romans considered it a charm against witchcraft and placed it in the cradles of infants. But it was the Serbian,

Croatian and Slavic traditions that most emphasized the use of hawthorn stakes against vampires.

As reported in Tony Thorne's book *Children of the Night: Of Vampires and Vampirism* (2000), in the early 1880s in the Slovakian village of Tomiselj, a man named Zirovec returned from the grave to harass his wife in bed, and pay "visits" to other neighbours. The priest and one of his colleagues decided to dig up the man in search of a *vedomec*. Having found sufficient evidence, they put a haw-thorn stake through his heart and reburied the corpse in another place. And in the 1882 case of a vampire in Varna, Bulgaria (reported by Ivanichka Georgieva in her 1985 book *Bulgarian Mythology*), after opening up the grave of an *oustrelli* suspected of causing an outbreak of disease and finding the body full of fresh blood, expert vampire hunters stuck a thorn from the tree into the breast of the corpse and then cremated the body on a fire of hawthorn branches. But before you mail-order some hawthorn for your own vampire dispatch kit, consider this note from Friedrich S. Krauss's 1892 book *South Slavic Countermeasures Against Vampires*: "The hawthorn must have been grown in the high mountains in a place from which the bush could not have seen the sea." So, you know, ask for that.

In modern cinema, one of the most memorable uses of hawthorn is in the otherwise dreadful Hammer film *The Satanic Rites of Dracula* (1973). In his speech about vampires, Professor Van Helsing (Peter Cushing) includes the tree in his list of weapons to be used against them. And—how convenient!—in the final chase scene through the woods with Christopher Lee's Count Dracula, Van Helsing runs right into a hawthorn bush! After getting his coat snagged on some thorns, he concocts a plot to lure Dracula into the bush to his death. And since this is a pretty hokey film, it actually works. The mighty Dracula struggles through the tree's brambles, bleeding and moaning all the way, and ultimately is trapped. He trips and falls to the ground, his head wrapped in a crown of thorns. Then Van Helsing pulls a post from a handy nearby fence free and stakes him to death. Silly? Yup. Dramatic? You bet.

Regardless of the type of wood used, the magical wooden stake has become a staple of vampire death scenes, making the jump from the oldest folktales right up to today's pop culture. You might even say stakes now have as much staying power as the vamps themselves. And it's probably thanks to the influence of one novel: *Varney the Vampyre*. First appearing in 1847 in the form of very popular, and very cheap pamphlets (the so-called penny dreadfuls), these weekly serials had recurring characters and repeated a lot of information ad nauseam, like a modern TV soap opera. So in practically every installment of Varney we find him being chased by angry mobs, who spend a lot of time discussing what they'd do if they actually caught up with him. One woman's take: "Drive a stake through him . . . It's the only way, and the humanest. You've only to take a hedge stake, and sharpen it a bit at one end, and char it a little in the fire so as there mayt'n't be no splinters to hurt, and then poke it through his stomach." Coming after John Polidori's "The Vampyre" but before Bram Stoker's *Dracula*, *Varney*'s surely the first story of note to use the historical accounts of vampirism that had been published in the early 1800s as the basis for a fictional gothic horror story.

Bram Stoker also researched superstitions about vampires, particularly the folklore of Transylvania, and much of his classic *Dracula* is based on actual legends and practices. For a century, *Dracula* was considered the go-to source for information about vampires, their powers and weaknesses, and stakes figure prominently in it, as expected. Professor Van Helsing carries a round wooden stake in his little black bag; the diary of Dr. Seward describes it thusly: "some two and a half or three inches thick and about three feet long. One end of it was hardened by charring in the fire, and was sharpened to a fine point." He also packed a heavy hammer "such as in households is used in the coal cellar for breaking the lumps." These are the tools used to stake the poor undead Lucy Westenra. The gruesome scene has often been described as a kind of gang rape on the woman's corpse. Van Helsing leads her three suitors—her fiancé Arthur Holmwood, Quincey Morris and Dr. Seward—to her coffin and instructs them on how to destroy the vampire Lucy and release the soul of the girl they love to true death. Arthur takes the stake and hammer, places the point over his beloved's heart and strikes down with all his might. Oh, how the vampire Lucy wailed and contorted but Arthur never faltered. As Stoker writes, "He looked like a figure of Thor as his untrembling arm rose and fell, driving deeper and deeper the mercy-bearing stake, whilst the blood from the pierced heart welled and spurted up around it." Later, Van Helsing also staked Dracula's three servant "brides" as they lay in their coffins. But when it came to the confrontation with Dracula himself, it was a slash of the throat and a stab to the heart that did in the infamous villain.

You'd be forgiven for feeling certain that Dracula met his end at the end of a pointy piece of wood though. In the classic Universal film adaptation of Stoker's novel, that is indeed what happens: Edward Van Sloan's Van Helsing grabs a makeshift stake (a piece of coffin wood) and a crowbar and attacks Bela Lugosi's Count Dracula. The scene was based on the stage play of the novel, in which Jonathan Harker does the deed in the presence of Van Helsing and others. In both the play and film, the audience does not actually see the staking. Censors demanded such a scenario be removed from the theatrical production and so the characters instead gather around the coffin, blocking the view. The film followed suit, with the killing blows heard but not pictured on-screen. In the bowels of the Count's spooky Carfax Abbey, Van Helsing locates Dracula resting in his coffin, then instructs Jonathan Harker to go find him something to help with the staking. The camera actually wanders off with Harker while we hear what can only be presumed to be the fatal blows, for, incredibly, we never see Dracula again. Indeed this may be the least exciting vampire movie climax of all time!

As the squeamishness of censors relaxed, some of the more recent adaptations have featured rather memorable stakings. (Hammer's *Dracula A.D. 1972* ramps things up a notch by having Christopher Lee's Dracula fall into a dirt pit filled with stakes, fatally impaling himself.)

In *'Salem's Lot*, Stephen King paints staking in much more horrific detail than Stoker ever did. His hero Ben Mears is not a professional slayer. He's a writer, returned to his hometown of Jerusalem's Lot to work on a book project. But when everyone in town starts to turn into vampires, it falls to him and a local priest, Father Callahan, to take action. In one scene starkly reminiscent of Arthur's staking of Lucy in *Dracula*, Mears must "free" his undead girlfriend Susan Norton by means of a staking to the heart as she sleeps. At Father Callahan's insistence, he takes a stake and a hammer and delivers the blows to her chest. Again and again and again. Susan does not go gently into that good night. Her eyes fly open. Her blood gushes forth, splashing Ben's face. Her body writhes. Her mouth emits a terrible, terrible shrieking, and spits out still more blood. As King writes, "His hands were scarlet, the stake was scarlet, the remorselessly rising and falling hammer was scarlet." Staking is a bloody business indeed.

Staking of a different, more sanitized kind was popularized in the modern era via TV's *Buffy the Vampire Slayer*. For heroine Buffy Summers, a wooden stake is kind of like AmEx: never leave home without it. She even has a "lucky stake" she affectionately calls Mr. Pointy. But she's not picky: she'll use whatever is handy. Over the course of the series, Buffy stakes vampires with, amongst other things, a picket fence post, a pool stick, a pumpkin patch sign, a shovel handle, a tree branch, and drumsticks. Quite contrary to *'Salem's Lot* and most horror films, staking here does not result in a gruesome display of blood spurting— Buffy's vamps simply turn to dust and blow away. This PG, low-rent approach fits Buffy's image as an ordinary girl with an extraordinary job. But she's not afraid to step it up a notch with a stake-shooting crossbow on occasion. (For a thought-provoking examination of Buffy's weapons and fighting style in the context of goddess mythology, I recommend Valerie Estelle Frankel's 2012 book *Buffy and the*

Heroine's Journey.) On the *Buffy* spin-off series *Angel*, there are even automatic stake-loaded wristbands, which conceal a stake under the slayer's clothing and are activated by a flex of the wrist. *The Vampire Diaries* TV show prioritizes the wood over the stake—including wooden bullets fired from a gun in the arsenal of weapons against vamps. (Wooden bullets really do exist, and have been used as training rounds in the military.) In the American indie horror film series *Subspecies* (1991–1998), a shotgun that fires wooden rosary beads is used. These kinds of innovations aren't unusual, and are welcomed by audiences; since the stake is such a hallmark of the genre, many writers have done their best to add an original spin to keep things interesting.

I Am Legend's protagonist Robert Neville makes his own wooden stakes in his shop to slay vamps as they sleep. A scientist, he is determined to solve the mystery of the undead, and his experiments conclude that vampirism is a virus that affects the anaerobic system. He posits that staking opens up the skin and introduces oxygen into the system, which destroys the bacteria and thus the vampire. If the stake is removed, however, the wound can heal. This fits into the folklore which claims the stake must remain in the vampire lest it reanimate, which Summers' *The Vampire, His Kith and Kin* calls a "highly important" detail.

Staking is such a cliché that it can be used as a visual punchline. In the horror-comedy *Vamp* (1986), a newly turned vampire pulls a stake from his chest and explains to his confused friends that it didn't kill him because it was made of Formica. A similar, albeit unintentionally funny, scene occurs in the Hammer film *Dracula Has Risen from the Grave* when Count Dracula (Christopher Lee) is staked in the heart but is able to pull the stake out. Much blood gushes from the wound as he tosses the oversized wooden stake like a javelin at his attacker and then runs off. How could this be? The local priest tells the attacker, a self-proclaimed non-believer, "You must pray or he won't die!" Ultimately, Dracula falls and is impaled on a giant cross, and since the priest appears to say a prayer while this is happening, it effectively destroys the vampire, his eyes bleeding, voice crying out, body dissolving to red dust. This scene could thus be considered an example of using sacred objects to kill your vampire, but it's also a caution against putting all your pointy pieces of wood in one basket.

So staking rituals evolve. One way modern fiction has updated the rules is by focusing specifically on piercing the heart. Vampire slayers need to practice hitting that sweet spot. Destruction of the heart has become so important that sometimes the staking itself is secondary, or even non-existent. On *The Vampire Diaries*, heart "extraction" is one way to kill absolutely everyone, including witches, werewolves and all manner of vamps and hybrids. You literally just reach in with your supernaturally strong hands and pull the beating, bloody organ out. Ta-da! (In one weird twist on this, a vampire in *Buffy* voluntarily had his heart surgically removed so that he would be temporarily invincible and able to go on a revenge killing spree in the sunlight.) Ripping out your foe's heart sounds like fun, but it's definitely a tactic best left for vamp-on-vamp battles, or experienced slayers only.

In David Wellington's vampire novels, the cop/slayer Laura Caxton learns that stakes don't work on vampires, because their skin is so thick it functions like a suit of armour. Her failed attempt at staking is described in *13 Bullets* (2006): "With all of her strength she brought it down, sharp end first, right into the vampire's ribcage, right into that white skin like carved marble. It might as well have been stone she attacked. The stake shivered all the way up its length, driving long splinters into the meat of her hand. Its point splayed out, twisted and broken." After that, Caxton carries a firearm. A Beretta 92, to be precise. Sometimes she uses bullets with a cross cut into the nose, not for sacred protection but because the slug breaks apart in the target, like shrapnel. In Wellington's world, vampires can regenerate in an instant, even from shots to the head. It's the heart that must be destroyed, by any means necessary. In one memorable scene from *13 Bullets*, Caxton's mentor, Arkeley, improvises with an electric jackhammer: "Strips of skin and then bits of muscle tissue like cooked chicken sputtered out of the wound. The vampire screamed with a noise she could hear just fine over the stuttering racket of the power tool and then . . . and then it was over. The vampire's head fell back and his mouth fell open and he was dead. Truly dead."

All of this experimentation fits right into the vampire killing tradition. Staking may have been the easiest, the fastest and most popular way to attack a vampire, but there was no surefire guarantee it would rid your village of the undead. In fact, more often than not, after digging up a grave and plunging a pointed weapon into the body, if you really wanted to be sure it would never come back to haunt you, it was time for even more drastic measures . . .

II. DECAPITATION

"I mean to decapitate the monster . . . To strike her head off . . .
with a hatchet, with a spade, or with anything that can cleave
through her murderous throat."
—General Spielsdorf, *Carmilla*

Instant brain death. That's what you get when you sever the head from the body. This is not why decapitation is so important in the slaying of vampires, of course, since they are already dead. But if you have tried your trusty wooden stake to the heart and found your vampire troubles haven't ceased, more severe action must be taken, and in folklore as well as fiction, beheading the suspect was the (un)natural next step.

Decapitation has been used as a means of capital punishment in cultures all over the world for centuries. In the strong hands of a professional executioner, a sharp axe or sword can easily sever the head with one strike, offering a quick and painless, if gruesome, death. Putting the head on public display afterwards served as a harsh reminder of the consequences of defiance of the law. The French perfected beheading with their guillotine, which became the only legal method to inflict the death penalty in that country from the French Revolution right up until 1977.

For an amateur, hacking off the head of a living human is not such an easy task. (I think this is probably a good thing.) I learned from my conversation with forensic anthropologist Myriam Nafte that even a fresh cadaver requires strength and skill, and a sharp implement, to slice through the strong muscles around the neck. See, for one example, Mary Queen of Scots, who required three blows and then an axe to take her royal head off. But after some decomposition, as muscle tissue breaks down, beheading becomes much easier. (In fact, a skull will easily detach from a dead body if it's left out in the open to rot.) So it's no surprise that suspected vampires were generally not decapitated at the time of burial, but some weeks or even months later. Usually this happened after staking proved unsatisfactory, although sometimes both methods were employed in tandem. Typically, the attackers would use a spade or a hoe, something already hanging around the cemetery, with a sharp edge and a long handle to distance themselves from any blood spatter. By removing the head, they hoped to truly put an end to the vampire's ability to rise from the grave.

The practice of decapitating or dismembering a body to prevent resurrection pre-dates the vampire superstition and has been observed around the world; Montague Summers noted the Ovambo tribe (of Namibia and Angola) cuts off the head (as well as severs the arms and legs) of dead magicians, for one example, while Michael E. Bell points out in *Food for the Dead: On the Trail of New England's Vampires* (2011) that a number of ancient Celtic burial sites have been uncovered where multiple skeletons are missing the skull. But as a means to destroy a vampire, decapitation was particularly popular amongst the European Slavs.

The earliest written account of a vampire decapitation comes from a 1689 publication by Slovenian scholar and nobleman Johann Valvasor, who reported on the case of one George Grando of Kringa (a village in present-day Croatia). As the story goes, in 1672 Grando died and was buried. But his widow claimed he was still tormenting her in the night, trying to suck her blood. Stories also began to circulate of a mysterious man roaming the village after dark, knocking on doors. When people began to die in the houses at which the spirit figure had called, the local chief magistrate deduced it must be George, as a vampire. He called together some of the villagers, got them drunk and then the angry mob went after Grando's grave, torches a-blazing. When they dug him up and discovered a corpse with a smile on its face and rosy cheeks, they were horrified and ran off to get a priest. But when they returned with a sharpened hawthorn stick and tried to drive it through the body, the wood reportedly rebounded from the flesh. Not until a man jumped up, grabbed a hoe and cut off Grando's head did the vampire "die"—with a loud shriek, contortion of the limbs and a massive spurt of blood. The mysterious deaths stopped. Grando's tale has become widely circulated in recent years, so much so that the town of Kringa now advertises the legend to attract tourists. At one point, a vampire-themed bar even opened. Should you find yourself in that neck of the woods, you can see Grando's actual grave, as he's buried in the cemetery of Saints Peter and Paul Church.

After the dastardly deed was done, the vampire was usually reburied, often in the same grave. But in order to prevent the body from simply reattaching its head, or carrying it around (it was believed that the head might possibly direct the body, even if severed), one was wise to further separate the two. Graves have been found containing heads placed between the knees of the corpses, or kept apart from the rest of the body by a layer of dirt, or even buried in a different location. This was particularly important when dealing with the *nachzehrer*, a German shroud-eating vampire. In the late 1800s, a *nachzehrer* case was reported in West Prussia. Soon after a woman named Gehrke died, her husband and children fell seriously ill and the townsfolk got suspicious. Her brother decided to open up her grave and what he saw compelled him to decapitate his sister's corpse with a spade. He placed the head under her arm and reburied the pieces. Interestingly, the man was later arrested for the crime and handed a jail sentence. He made an appeal for self-defence and the charge was thrown out. A similar case occurred in 1870 in the town of Kantrzyno (in present-day Poland). A man called Franz von Poblocki died, and shortly after so did his son Anton. While Anton's corpse was still waiting to be buried, other family members began to suffer from health problems and horrible nightmares. The family came to the conclusion that old Franz had become a vampire, so they hired a local vampire expert to decapitate Anton and bury him with his head between his legs. They also dug up and decapitated the father's corpse. For his efforts, the vampire hunter was put on trial and received a four-month sentence.

Despite growing unease about this kind of desecration of the body amongst government officials and law enforcement, would-be vampire hunters continued to wield the spade wherever superstitions flared up.

Numerous accounts of chopped-off vampire heads from across Europe throughout the 1700s and 1800s were published, becoming a field of study for folklorists, historians and even theologians, whose publications went on to serve as research material for novelists and playwrights. But no decapitation tale of the era has influenced modern vampire mythology as much as what went down in Liebava.

A Hungarian travelling through the village of Liebava, Moravia (in present-day Czech Republic), was told that a pesky revenant had been haunting the community for four years. A self-styled vampire expert, the traveller declared he could destroy the creature. From his lookout above the church one night, he observed the vampire rise from the grave, take off its cloth shroud and then go out, presumably to bother the townsfolk. The stranger climbed down and gathered up the cloth, and took it with him back up the church steeple. When the vampire returned to find his shroud missing, he was pissed and, after much taunting from the Hungarian, climbed up to the top of the church to retrieve his shroud. What happened next varies by account: either the Hungarian threw him off the stairs, or he smacked him hard with a spade, causing him to slip. Either way the vampire suffered a great fall—after which the stranger leapt down and cut his head off with the spade. The villagers reported no further hauntings.

This story was originally reported by a priest who was called to Liebava to hear testimony from the villagers about what had happened. It later appeared in Augustin Calmet's *The Phantom World*. It's this version I suspect was a direct influence on the Irish writer Sheridan Le Fanu.

Le Fanu's *Carmilla* is widely recognized as one of the most notable and influential of all vampire tales. The story is told from the point of view of Laura, a young English girl living in a castle in remote Styria (part of Austria) who receives a strange visitor in the alluring Carmilla. The two become fast friends but Carmilla exhibits some rather unusual behaviour: sleeping all day, sleepwalking all night, and making sexual advances on her innocent host, who starts experiencing nightmares and then becomes mysteriously ill. Laura's concerned father meets with his friend General Spielsdorf, who explains how his niece recently died under similar circumstances in the company of the same woman (though she calls herself Mircalla). The two eventually unravel Carmilla's true identity as Countess Karnstein—a vampire. The General explains, "There remains to me but one object which can interest me during the few years that remain to me on Earth, and that is to wreak on her the vengeance which, I thank God, may still be accomplished by a mortal arm. I mean to decapitate the monster."

Where did Le Fanu get his idea that Carmilla should be decapitated? From the Liebava vampire legend, presumably. For within his story he practically quotes the whole thing. When looking for the ruined Castle Karnstein, Laura and company encounter an axeman in the woods who tells them of a Moravian nobleman who killed a vampire there long ago. His details are familiar: the travelling stranger, church steeple, stealing of shroud, and how "the Moravian, with a stroke of his sword, clove his skull in twain, hurling him down to the churchyard, wither, descending by the winding stairs, the stranger followed and cut his head off . . ."

It's obvious why the Liebava tale would appeal to a

writer. It's one of the few historical vampire accounts where the bloodsucker is actually confronted in action. Although nobody but the hunter himself actually witnessed its rise from the grave, the image of the fight scene, a dramatic fall and a beheading was ripe for use in fiction. The story of *Carmilla* takes it a step further, climaxing with a death by staking and a head chopped off, from which "a torrent of blood flowed." These gory details, not to mention the titillation of lesbian eroticism, has made *Carmilla* a favourite for modern film adaptations, notably Roger Vadim's *Blood and Roses* (1960) and Hammer's Karnstein Trilogy, which includes *The Vampire Lovers* (1970), starring Ingrid Pitt as the vampire and Peter Cushing as General von Spielsdorf. The latter opens and closes with decapitations I would call rather graphic for the pre-slasher era of horror: the opening scene is an exciting dramatization of the steeple/shroud story, with a Baron Joachim von Hartog taking on a beautiful, blonde bloodsucker, sword in hand. As she attempts to plunge her fangs into his neck we see him strike out with the blade, grabbing onto her hair as he slices the head off; later Cushing destroys Carmilla with a big, long stake to the heart followed by a sword beheading. "There's no other way," he explains. In a departure from Le Fanu's story (which ends with Carmilla's body being burned and the ashes thrown into a river), these vampire hunters put the beheaded vampire back into its tomb. Case—and coffin—closed. (Until the sequel, that is.)

Elements of *Carmilla* also permeate Bram Stoker's *Dracula*, written two decades later, particularly in the seductive depiction of the undead Lucy, and the remote eastern European location of the Count's castle. (Stoker's research notes show the author originally set *Dracula* in Styria, then changed it to Transylvania.) Stoker also subscribed to the practice of decapitating vampires. Professor Van Helsing shocks Lucy's suitor Dr. Seward when, upon her death, he declares his intention to "cut off her head and take out her heart." When the time comes, and Lucy is staked, he makes good on his promise, then fills her mouth with garlic and seals up the coffin once more. Later, he takes on the "butcher work" of staking and decapitating Dracula's three brides as they rest in their coffins. (Strangely, before he could behead the master vampire himself, Dracula, having been staked in the heart and slashed at the throat, crumbles into dust.)

Even had Stoker used decapitation as his climax for *Dracula*, it's unlikely that scene would have made it into the many stage and cinema versions that followed. As previously noted, in the early 1900s even the stakings were done off-screen, to not offend the sensibilities of the audience. By the 1970s, however, those glorious Hammer films had upped the ante for gore, and the slasher boom of the 1980s set the stage for much bloodier cinematic fare. And so we find a Dracula for the modern age in the Francis Ford Coppola version, *Bram Stoker's Dracula*. Even though we still don't see Lucy beheaded on-screen, and the final fight scene sticks to the death-by-knife-wound storyline of the novel, Coppola uses decapitation in a truly memorable fashion in his ending. His film features a love story between Dracula (Gary Oldman) and Mina (Winona Rider) and at the end, after the Count is stabbed with a dagger and falls to the ground, she rushes to him. As Dracula's face reverse-ages from shrivelled beast to handsome young prince, Mina plunges the dagger further into his chest. Then she kisses him. He seems to be at peace. But wait! Mina then yanks the dagger from his body and swiftly beheads him with it. In Stoker's novel, the character of Mina exhibits some serious slayer potential, playing an important role in hunting down Dracula, but in films she's usually relegated to being a victim while Van Helsing and his male sidekicks take on the monster. Here then, she is finally given a chance to star in the heroic ending as the ultimate vampire lover/killer.

Since then, we've seen the rise of the horror/action hybrid, heavy on CGI monsters and high-energy fight scenes. Gory vampire decapitations have fit right in, although not necessarily in the traditional folkloric sense. Now we have full-on martial arts sequences in flicks like *Blade* and *Blood: The Last Vampire* (2009), where samurai swords, not sexton's spades, are the weapons of choice. And as vampires went more PG in the 2000s, horror filmmakers looking to bring back the fright factor often turned to graphic beheadings to do it.

One of the best and most horrific vampire films of the 2000s is *30 Days of Night* (2007), adapted from the comic book by American Steve Niles and Australian Ben Templesmith. A clan of vampires attacks the northern town of Barrow, Alaska, just as it's beginning a winter month of complete darkness. ("We should have come here ages ago," says one.) These vamps are monstrous, true *nosferatu*-like creatures, and they are immune to garlic, bullets, staking and the like. Only direct sunlight or beheading can kill them, and since there won't be any sun for 30 days, the townsfolk who want to survive have to get used to taking off some heads, even if those heads are attached to an innocent-looking but bloodthirsty young girl, or a former best friend. These kill scenes are some of the most memorable in the film. Decapitation serves another purpose in *30 Days of Night* as well: separating heads from bodies prevents those who died of a vampire bite from coming back from the dead. While the film's emotional climax focuses on the harm done by sunlight (more on that soon), the concept of decapitation as a means of destruction is well used here.

Some of the nastiest decapitations in modern vampire film happen in the Twilight movies. In Stephenie Meyer's vampire saga, bloodsuckers are immune to stakes, sunlight and other traditional weapons. But they can die from being ripped to pieces, and they seem to be quite good at literally biting the heads off their undead enemies, or even tearing them apart with bare hands. So in the big-budget films (particularly in the final chapter, *Breaking Dawn — Part 2*), CGI vampire heads roll, fly through the air and otherwise make a rather awful mess. And since the Golden Rule of Twilight is that the existence of vampires must be kept a secret, these heads and body parts are then burned.

That's the thing about decapitation. For all its effectiveness for both practical and dramatic reasons, it has a drawback: now you have vampire parts to dispose of. As noted above, in the old days people simply reburied the head and body separately and that would be the end of it. But if you want to be extra certain you will never see that vampire again, you set the corpse to flame.

III. FIRE

"'Fire purifies . . .' Claudia said. And I said, 'No, fire merely destroys. . . .'" — Louis, *Interview with the Vampire*

Death is a contagion. Undeath, perhaps even more so. So to "kill" the vampire by staking, or even decapitation and dismemberment, leaves the problem of what to do with the body, lest it continue to infect the innocent. Film and television writers have developed convenient plot devices to erase the threat of reanimation or spread: disintegrating vampires with special effects means final death. On *Buffy the Vampire Slayer*, a staked vampire immediately turns to dust; on *True Blood*, they explode into gooey bits. But in folklore, getting rid of a mostly intact vampire corpse usually required some additional effort—burning.

Cremation of corpses is not unusual, or in any way supernatural. It predates burial, being a regular practice amongst ancient Greeks and Romans as well as Hindus, pagans and others throughout the world. When Christians took over the Roman Empire, they outlawed cremation, but it's practical and hygienic. For some, it also signifies the release of the soul from the body—a desirable state— which in terms of vampires makes it good for the living (as protection) and the dead (as peace). And so even if Orthodox Catholics didn't want to burn vampires, traditional attitudes about cremation persisted. According to Paul Barber's *Vampires, Burial, and Death*, some Bulgarians around the Black Sea pre-emptively burned all of their dead so that "they would not become vampires." In Greece, finding a hole in the dirt around a grave is sign a vampire lies within, and they would sometimes put a fire into the hole instead of bothering with exhumation. And for most cultures throughout Europe, if nothing else worked, the one surefire way to destroy a vampire was annihilation through cremation, a theory that is emphasized again and again in some of the best-known historical accounts of vampirism.

The limitation of stakes and the value of fire are highlighted in the rather humorous case of the "Blow Vampire." The date of the incident is uncertain, some say as far back as 1336, but it has been documented repeatedly, starting with Charles Ferdinand de Schertz in his publication *Magia Postuma* (1704) and republished in Augustin Calmet's widely read dissertation on revenants and vampires from 1751. In the Bohemian village of Blow (or possibly "Blau," now part of the Czech Republic), a shepherd named Myslata died and was buried. His body was still seen every night in and around his village, terrorizing people; he would call them out by name, and within eight days they would die. When his corpse was finally exhumed from the ground and staked, he rose up and thanked his attackers for giving him a stick with which to defend himself against dogs! An executioner was then called in to stake him again. The vampire Myslata apparently cried out, moved its limbs and gushed blood. He was taken to a pyre outside the village and burned, after which the attacks stopped.

The detail of the body being burned away from the village is not insignificant: as with any contagion, the objective was often to put as much distance between the vampire and victims as possible. We see variations on this theme throughout folkloric accounts.

The legend of the so-called Silesia Shoemaker further illustrates the common practice of using one method and then another to rid a community of a vampire. As reported by Henry More in his *Antidote Against Atheism* (1653), a shoemaker in Breslau, Silesia (now called Wroclaw, in present-day Poland), committed suicide in 1591. To avoid shame, his family concealed that fact and gave him a proper burial. But rumours of his suicide persisted, as did reports of his creeping about at night, "pinching and suffocating" people. Seven months after his burial, his body was dug up and found to be not yet decomposed. The townsfolk reburied it beneath the gallows, but the hauntings persisted. They then exhumed the body anew and cut it into pieces, severing the head, arms, legs, and removing the heart. They burned the parts in a fire, and then they threw the ashes in a river. The shoemaker vampire was never seen again. (A similar incident occurred in 1700 on the Greek island of Mykonos; see sidebar page 68.) One might ask why vampire hunters didn't simply go straight for the flame when dealing with an inconvenient or dangerous revenant, if it was so effective. The truth is cremation without a modern crematorium is expensive and not particularly quick. The human body, even after death, has a high water content; also, since fire needs oxygen, anywhere the body touches the ground will not burn. Thus, villagers would have needed a furnace and/or a lot of fuel, both of which may have been in short supply. To say nothing of the unpleasantness of having to stoke the corpse of a loved one for the many hours it would take to turn the body into fragments of bone and ash. Then there's the fear that the vampire could still escape. One of the most bizarre notions in all of vampire lore is that one could transform itself into smaller creatures that leap out of the flames and run away.

In his report *South Slavic Countermeasures Against Vampires* (1892), Friedrich S. Krauss notes that proper burial of a suspected vampire requires one group of people to tend to the body while others look out for any moths or butterflies flying away from the grave. If one is spotted, it must be captured and thrown into a bonfire. If the butterfly escapes or is not burned, the vampire will wreak vengeance for seven years.

In the Russian fairytale of the Soldier and the Vampire, a soldier returning home encounters an undead warlock in a cemetery, burning a great fire. The warlock invites the soldier to a wedding to drink and be merry. But the warlock then flies into a rage and attacks the bride and groom, piercing their hands with an awl and filling vials with their blood. He tells the soldier this will put them into a sleep only he can wake them from, with a ritual involving cutting them open and pouring their own blood back into the wounds. The soldier, with casual aplomb, enquires about how exactly one could destroy the mischievous undead warlock and learns it would take "a pyre of aspen boughs, a hundred loads of them." With one catch: "snakes and worms and different kinds of reptiles would creep out of my insides," says the warlock, "and crows and magpies and jackdaws would come flying up. All these must be caught and flung into the pyre. If so much as a single maggot were to escape, in that maggot, I should slip away." At the dawn of the cock's crow, the warlock falls lifeless. So, after rescuing the bride and groom using the ritual described above, the soldier gathers the villagers and they burn the warlock's body together, ensuring not a single maggot gets away. The ashes are strewn to the wind and from that time on the village is at peace.

When Bram Stoker was researching and writing *Dracula* in the 1890s, cremation was quite trendy across Europe, so it's surprising that the author makes no mention of it in his story. Fire had already made an appearance in the 1847 serial *Varney the Vampire*, which climaxed with Varney throwing himself into an active volcano to kill himself. But with few exceptions (e.g., in *Dracula's Daughter*, the Countess Marya burns Dracula's body to ashes and throws salt on it to destroy him), the use of fire as a dramatic tool didn't really take off until late in the 20th century.

By the early 1970s, Stoker's *Dracula* was already one of the most adapted novels ever published. Filmmakers were surely looking for new ways to thrill audiences so familiar with the plot. Oh, you could still stake Lucy and the Brides, maybe even show beheadings on-screen, but for the climax, when it came time to dispatch Count Dracula, why not try something original?

Spanish director Jess Franco's *Count Dracula* (1970), a film low on budget but heavy on cheese, sees Van Helsing (Herbert Lom) scare Dracula (Christopher Lee) away from Mina by drawing a cross of fire on the floor with a fireplace poker. Later, for the final confrontation, Jonathan

Harker and Quincey Morris intercept Dracula's coffin, pry it open and set it ablaze with a torch. In a cheap special effect, the face of Dracula is seen to age rapidly, then melt away to his skeleton, after which the hunters dump the flaming coffin from off the top of the castle, and it shatters on the road below. Cue end credits. Also that year, the hammy Hammer film *Scars of Dracula* sees the stake prove worthless against the Count (once again, Christopher Lee). A would-be slayer first uses a wood table leg as a stake, but Dracula simply hypnotizes the attacker until he faints; later, the attacker tries spearing Dracula through the chest with an iron bar, but he simply pulls it out with a smirk. The joke is on the Count though, because they are on top of a castle in a lightning storm! Still holding on to the iron rod, Dracula gets struck by lightning and catches fire, his skin blistering and blackening while he screams in agony before falling over the castle walls and plummeting in flames to his death below. Not to be outdone, 1971's *Lust for a Vampire*, based on Le Fanu's *Carmilla*, combines both staking and burning in one twist of a climax: when an angry mob sets upon the family of vampires hiding out in Castle Karnstein with torches, the priest tries to warn them, "Fire will not serve . . . nothing kills them but stakes or decapitation." They torch the building anyhow. The three vampires inside, including the young Mircalla/Carmilla, stand defiant in the face of the flames. Until a large wooden beam falls, on fire, from the ceiling and plunges into Mircalla's chest, pining her to the floor where she burns to ashes. End credits roll over the image of the castle burning.

Perhaps nobody has done more to cement fire as the preferred means of vampire destruction in modern times than Anne Rice. Her Vampire Chronicles series has so much fire in it the books practically self-combust. In the first novel alone, we see Louis torch his own family plantation, Claudia set fire to a doll shop and the entire Théâtre des Vampires go up in flames. After killing Lestat by poison (or so they believe) and dumping his body in a swamp, Louis and Claudia are shocked to see him return. "Do you believe that had we burned his remains he would have died?" Louis asks. "Of course I believe it. If there is nothing to rise, there is nothing to rise," offers Claudia. They get the chance to test their theory when their apartment catches fire and they leave the weakened Lestat there to meet his fate. Later, Louis asks the elder vampire Armand point blank what can kill them. "The destruction of your remains," answers Armand. "Fire, dismemberment, the heat of the sun. Nothing else."

Lestat knew this already: in his origin story, *The Vampire Lestat*, he tells of his master Magnus killing himself by leaping into a fire, but not before explaining to Lestat the importance of scattering his ashes afterwards, lest he should return, "and in what shape that would be I dare not contemplate." In that same novel, Armand forces members of his coven into a pyre; the master vampire Marius is set alight with 50 torches by an angry Satanic coven burning down his house; and we are introduced to the mighty queen vampire Akasha, who can conjure fire with her mind. As the Chronicles unfold over several books, Rice repeatedly returns to vampire death-by-fire, either for suicide or revenge. For the film adaptation of *Interview with the Vampire*, director Neil Jordan seized on the theme and

Rice's world comes alive in blazing shades of red, orange and gold.

Since Rice, other important vampire franchises have used fire prominently in their rulebooks. Chelsea Quinn Yarbro's fictional Count St. Germain explains in *Hôtel Transylvania*, that "true death" for vampires is only caused by fire or the severing of the spine. And in Stephenie Meyer's Twilight Saga, after a vampire is ripped apart, it's crucial to burn the remains before it reanimates. It will be interesting to see what long-term effect the popularity of these rules has on vampire storytelling in the 21st century. Some writers may choose to go in the completely opposite direction, or invent something totally original. But it's easy to imagine that the next generation of vampire readers will look upon burning as the go-to tactic, not a last resort.

IV. SUNLIGHT

"Sunlight fatal. Repeat: fatal. Would destroy them."
—Professor Van Helsing, *Horror of Dracula*

So far, all the ways cited to destroy a vampire have something in common: they would kill the living too. There's nothing about impaling the heart, chopping off a head or burning a body to a crisp that is exclusive to killing vampires or supernatural creatures. While there is sometimes magic in the ritual—in specifying that the stake be hawthorn, for example—and the entire vampire concept is based on superstition, for the most part the Old World traditions aren't particularly imaginative when it comes to ways to take out their monsters.

The idea that vampires can't go out in the sunlight doesn't come from folklore. It's true they've always been considered nocturnal, and historical accounts typically have them only sighted after sundown. But that is true of most boogeymen and, as outlined above, probably has as much to do with them being the product of nightmares as anything else.

Even fiction writers didn't dream up the idea. Nowhere in Bram Stoker's *Dracula* does it state the vampire dies at dawn. In fact, his vampire can move about by daylight, albeit with reduced powers. Nor did Polidori's Lord Ruthven or Le Fanu's Carmilla die from sunlight. No, the concept that sunlight itself is fatal to a vampire was created for the medium of film.

F.W. Murnau's 1922 film *Nosferatu,* the earliest surviving film adaptation of Bram Stoker's *Dracula*, is the origin of the sunlight myth, the first supernatural way to destroy a vampire. *Nosferatu* was written by Henrik Galeen, who "freely adapted" Stoker's novel for the screen, changing the character names and location, writing about the Transylvanian Count Orlok and setting the bulk of the action not in London, England, but in Wisborg, Germany. The story, at least the first half, will be familiar to anyone who has read *Dracula*: a young businessman (Thomas Hutter, the Jonathan Harker stand-in) is sent to a Transylvanian castle to meet with mysterious Count. Much has been made of Count Orlok's grotesque appearance, so different from the aristocratic style Bela Lugosi would bring to the role a decade later. The shooting script describes him as pale and ghostly with hollow eyes, a thin mouth and sharp, rat-like teeth. Actor Max Schreck brought Orlok to life as tall, thin and monstrous, with claw-like fingernails and fangs which are not canines but prominent front teeth, like a rat. All the better for Galeen's take on the vampire as a plague. The town of Wisborg is suffering from widespread plague and the arrival of the Count represents a different kind of threat than Dracula did in Whitby. Orlok is something much, much dirtier, and he's come not to seduce a few women but to infect the entire town with disease. (One theory on the origins of the word *nosferatu* is that it derives from the Greek *nosophoros*, meaning "plague carrier.")

There is no vampire hunting team in *Nosferatu*. Rather, Ellen Hutter (a.k.a. Mina Harker) is the heroine of the tale. Concerned about her husband Thomas's mysterious bite marks and illness since returning from Transylvania, she reads a book about vampires. She learns "Only a woman can break his frightful spell—a woman pure in heart—who will offer her blood freely to *nosferatu* and will keep the vampire by her side until after the cock has crowed." And so Ellen decides to lure Count Orlok to her bedside and, um, distract him, until the morning light. She sacrifices herself, not only out of love for her husband but for the good of a community she is sick of watching being carried away one by one in coffins. And when the *nosferatu* comes to her, creeping up the stairs, his long fingernails casting an eerie shadow on the wall, she welcomes him. In the early morning, just as he's about to feed on Ellen's neck, we hear the cock's crow and see the monster's face, full of terror at the realization that he's stayed up way past coffin-time. As the sun's rays creep in through the window, the Count stumbles, arms outstretched in disbelief, then clutches at his chest as the panic washes over him. The sun hits his body, and he simply fades away. Title card: "The master is dead!"

Oddly, the idea for the ending of *Nosferatu* is attributed to Murnau, not Galeen. The director apparently found the screenplay missing pages, and so rewrote parts of it on his own. His motivation for using sunlight to kill Count Orlok is not known—some film historians have suggested he was eager to use the cool new vanishing effect—but we do have the script note: "Nosferatu attempts to escape but is touched by the sunlight. He vanishes in a puff of smoke."

And just like that the rules for destroying a vampire were forever changed.

If you think about it, there could be a logical, scientific reason for why sunlight would harm the undead. I turn again to the book *Flesh and Bone* by forensic anthropologist Myriam Nafte. It lists the environmental variables affecting decomposition of dead bodies, noting that in cold, dry climates the process is slowed down. It also explains that frozen bodies, once thawed, decompose much more rapidly than fresh ones. Since much of the vampire legend originates from eastern European countries with long, cold winters (Romania, Slovakia, Bulgaria, etc.), presumably many a suspected vampire was buried in cold, dry ground and would have frozen. And so not only would they, once exhumed, appear to be less decomposed than they should be—number one proof of vampirism—but when exposed to the elements, the corpse would start to break down very quickly. Okay, not instantaneously as in *Nosferatu*. But sunlight, being heat, does accelerate decomposition. And so if a body was truly undead, the process of cellular breakdown already started but somehow held in suspended animation through supernatural forces, could, with exposure to a burst of bright sunlight, cause serious harm and rapid decay. Hey, it's a theory.

But no matter the reason why sunlight is fatal to some vampires, it's become fully entrenched in the lore now, the shadow of Murnau's invention looming large over the mythology for decades, with no signs of stopping.

As early as 1943's *Son of Dracula*, we see sunlight introduced as a means to destroy vampires. Lon Chaney Jr. as Count Alucard (Dracula spelled backwards, ha ha) is killed when his coffin is dragged outside and burned, leaving the Count nowhere to hide when the dawn comes. The rays of the sun reduce him to skeleton, and a close-up of his hand shows the flesh fade away, leaving only bone and a ring on its finger. Film historians claim this was the first time audiences saw a special effect of flesh disintegrating, and it certainly caught on. A year later, *The Return of the Vampire* finds the vampire Armand Tesla (Bela Lugosi) being dragged, unconscious, into the daylight by a werewolf servant (don't ask) named Andreas. It's unclear if Andreas actually knows he's dooming his ex-master to true death; nevertheless, the vampire's face melts away from exposure to the sun, an effect so disturbing at the time that British censors had the ending changed, approving ye old classic staking instead. Yet another Universal Studios Dracula picture, 1945's *House of Dracula*, also ignores the rules set out by Stoker; copying *The Return of the Vampire*, Count Dracula (John Carradine) is destroyed when his coffin is dragged out at sunrise and its lid opened. He fades to a skeleton.

By the time the U.K.'s Hammer Films released *Horror of Dracula* in 1958, sunlight was so ingrained in the mythology that Professor Van Helsing is absolutely emphatic about it, declaring vampires allergic to light and reading into his diary report, "Sunlight fatal. Repeat: fatal. Would destroy them." Later, in a memorable climax, after Van Helsing chases Dracula back to his castle and the two men circle each other like fencers for a while, the slayer leaps heroically onto a banquet table and throws himself at the heavy velvet curtains, pulling them down and letting sunlight spill through the stained glass windows. He then crafts a makeshift crucifix by holding two candlesticks in the shape of a cross, which repels Dracula and pushes him into the sun's rays, where he falls and burns. This scene would be repeated often, such as in *Bram Stoker's Dracula* (1973) directed by Dan Curtis, 1979's *Dracula* directed by John Badham and the 1979 remake of *Nosferatu* by Werner Herzog, which uses both sunlight and staking.

The '80s horror/comedy *Fright Night* pays homage to the iconic scenario. In the climax of the film, TV horror host turned (rather impotent) vampire hunter Peter Vincent (Roddy McDowell) and newbie slayer Charley Brewster (William Ragsale) confront the ruthless vampire Jerry Dandridge (Chris Sarandon) in a basement. Their stakes prove useless but Charley starts smashing all the windows and letting the sunlight in, then uses a mirror to reflect concentrated rays on Dandridge until he bursts into flames. (When his skin falls off, it reveals his skeleton to be a giant bat, for some reason.)

Clearly, there's a lot of potential for dramatic scenes with death-by-sunlight. And since the vamp bursts immediately into flames, there's no need for any reburial or special funeral pyre or other disposal; the corpse simply disappears, allowing the remaining characters to get on with the plot. At first, screenwriters reserved this tool for dispatching the lead villain: you would still stake Lucy or the Brides or any lesser vamps in their coffins, but when it came for the climactic showdown with the Count or other master vampire, sunlight was the shiny new weapon of choice.

An interesting thing happened in the 1980s: the sun became a weapon of mass destruction. This was partly in response to the evolution of vampire storytelling. We didn't just have one vampire anymore, or even a master vampire and a few minions. We now had families of vampires, entire societies of vampires. In our books and films, we needed to kill hordes of them at once. Meanwhile in real life, the public became more aware of problems with the Earth's ozone layer, the thing that protects humans from the sun's deadly UV rays. It was being depleted. Skin cancers due to UV radiation were on the rise. The ozone above the Antarctic had a hole in it. It is in this context, when governments were banning CFC-emitting aerosol cans and humans were slathering on more SPF, that the sun started to feel pretty dangerous. And as always, vampire stories changed to keep pace with our fears. If the sun was going to hurt us now, well, at least we could fantasize about using it to destroy our enemies too.

For their part, fictional vampires adapted nicely to the new threat with survival tactics of their own. The 1987 western/horror hybrid *Near Dark* (directed by Kathryn Bigelow) had its cowboy bloodsuckers black out their vehicles with spray paint and tinfoil for emergency daytime use, and carry blankets to throw over their bodies when caught outside, for they would smoke and blister if exposed. The film's finale sees the vamps literally racing against the sunrise. In that memorable scene, one character runs down the middle of a road in mid-morning sun, skin smoking and blackening until he bursts into flames and explodes. In the 2010 Australian futuristic horror film *Daybreakers*, vampires run the world and have designed high-end sun-proof cars to drive during daylight hours.

In the book and TV series *The Vampire Diaries*, sunlight burns and is fatal, but lead characters Stefan and Damon Salvatore (as well as other key vamps) walk about freely at all hours—thanks to "daylight rings." Crafted by witches with a closely guarded spell and a lapis lazuli gemstone, the ring provides the wearer (and only the specific vampire it was created for) protection from both the harmful rays and public suspicion: anyone seen in midday can't possibly be a vampire, right? The ring also allows *TVD*'s writers an opportunity to create heightenened drama around the threat of sun exposure. Rings can be removed—a means to vampire murder, or even suicide. In one memorable incident, a vampire lucky enough to possess a daylight ring was compelled to remove it while standing in a cemetery in broad daylight; up in flames she went, meeting her final death before her own gravestone.

In the 1990 novel *Vampire$* by John Steakley, slayer Jack Crow and his team at Vampire$ Inc. have developed unique tactics to hunt their prey (who, incidentally, are looking for a relic that will give them the ability to walk in the daytime). They use crossbows, winches and pickup trucks to drag vampires out from their lairs into the sunlight, where they burn to their deaths. "She went into something beyond hideous when the sunlight struck her," writes Steakley of one dispatched vamp. "The thing in the flame was no longer recognizable as anything but a roaring blue and white fire. There came a loud hissing sound, as though gas was escaping. Then sparks. Then a loud pop. Then the flame was gone. Everything was gone save for a foot-wide circle of ashes." This horrific imagery of burning vampires was made even more gruesome in the 1998 film adaptation directed by master of horror John Carpenter. James Woods as Jack Crow does the old tearing-down-the-curtains trick one better by ripping the entire roof off a wooden barn where he's fighting the master vamp. The villain has nowhere to hide and bursts into flames and explodes into gory, gooey pieces.

Anne Rice's use of fire also extends to sunlight. In the film version of *Interview with the Vampire*, director Neil Jordan doesn't hold back in depicting the cruel punishment of Claudia for betraying the vampire rules of law and killing another vamp. (In Rice's world, there are no slayers; humans barely know of the undead's existence, never mind how to destroy them.) Claudia and her mother figure, Madeleine, are imprisoned in a tower in the Théâtre des Vampires and left to burn in the sun as it passes overhead. The sensitive Louis finds their remains locked in a final embrace, a horrifyingly beautiful sculpture of black ash that crumbles at his touch. Rice plays with expanding the sunlight mythology in her novel *Queen of the Damned* (1988). Older vampires are somewhat immune to sunlight, and there is that small matter of what happens when the master vampires Akasha and Enkil are exposed to the sun: it kills all vampires worldwide.

Here we start to see the development of complex rules involving sunlight, to suit the needs of writers handling more than just one novel or screenplay, but instead having to craft an entire series of books or seasons of a TV show. Since sunlight-as-weapon is purely a fictional construct with no basis in folklore, writers can really do as they please without any concern for alleged authenticity. And when it comes to TV, they do a lot.

In the series *True Blood*, which premiered in 2008 and is based on the Southern Vampire Mysteries novels by American Charlaine Harris, vamps can still be killed by traditional methods—staking, decapitation, fire—but "meeting the sun" is a particularly nasty way to go, and is often used for suicide. Around the same time *True Blood* debuted, the BBC series *Being Human* (a vampire, a werewolf and a ghost share a flat) was also playing with sunlight in its storylines. While most of its vampires can walk about in the day, they are sensitive to sunlight and cover themselves in appropriate protective clothing. This is an evolution from the time of the elders when sunlight was deadlier. And so, as writers adapt, so do their creations.

Funnily enough, one of the best modern vampire films to use sunlight as a plot point got its own origin wrong. In *30 Days of Night*, Alaskan townsfolk under attack determine that sunlight can hurt vampires—but they are in a month of complete darkness. So they devise a plan to use a UV lamp as a weapon. At one point, a character quips, "Just because something stopped Bela Lugosi doesn't mean it can stop these things." We know that sunlight was never used against Bela's Count Dracula, but this is proof of just how much even hardcore genre junkies who get paid to write horror movies consider it part of the original vampire myth.

They were on to something with the UV lamp though. F.W. Murnau could not have predicted how the future of vampire storytelling would evolve to include the weaponization of sunlight. But as it turns out, UV has had a very strong role to play in the action/adventure-heavy vampire films of the modern age.

In the popular film franchise Underworld, in which a race of werewolves fight against vampires, each side has developed weapons that target their enemy's weaknesses: vampires have the advantage with silver bullets until the werewolves develop ultraviolet ammunition. Introduced in 2003's *Underworld*, these hollow bullets are filled with an irradiated fluid that emits UV light. "Daylight harnessed as a weapon," notes one vampire. They also glow in the dark and look pretty cool.

These kinds of high-tech anti-vamp toys are also featured heavily in the Blade movies. In *Blade II*, Blade, a half-vampire who hunts his own kind for revenge, is packing UV flashbang grenades. At various points in the film trilogy we also see his car modified to have UV headlights, a UV-laser weapon and bullets with built-in UV called Sun Dogs that melt vampires from the inside out, with all the CGI blood and fire a blockbuster budget can create.

All this special effects wizardry has done nothing to take away from the simple, striking image that started it all: a vampire silently fading to nothingness against the backdrop of a rising sun. What *Nosferatu* created in 1922 can never be undone.

V. SILVER

Silver kills werewolves, everyone knows that. But it can
also weaken or kill vampires, something that is often over-
looked or even disputed. It's no surprise there is confusion
around its use against different supernatural creatures
though, as debate about the harmful versus helpful properties of silver exists in the real world too.

Silver kills bacteria and it has thus been used for a
long time by the medical profession, as an antiseptic in
wound dressings for example. Plenty of metals have this
effect, but silver is considered the least toxic for humans.
However, silver nitrate *is* caustic and corrosive and will
burn and blacken the skin. And yet, to confuse matters
further, colloidal silver—a solution of silver compounds
in water created by electrolysis—has recently been trum-
peted as an alternative health treatment for strengthening
the immune system. Some question its benefits and point
to the danger of argyria, an irreversible condition caused
by exposure to silver chemicals. Argyria turns the skin
blue-grey and makes one very, very sensitive to sunlight.

Hmmm . . . and isn't silver used in mirrors and in photography, two things most vampires avoid like the plague? Intriguing indeed. But since silver is not known to be lethal to human beings, whatever logic around why it would be able to destroy a vampire exists purely in the realm of the magical.

There are few references to silver in vampire folklore. Montague Summers writes in his *The Vampire, His Kith and Kin* how in some Slavic countries there is a belief that vampires can be killed if shot with a silver bullet blessed by a priest—as long as the body is not exposed to moonlight, especially a full moon, in which case it will rise with "redoubled vigour and malevolence." And Paul Barber's *Vampires, Burial, and Death* references a Serbian who claimed a silver coin with a cross on it could, if broken into pieces and loaded into a shotgun shell, kill a vampire.

Bram Stoker made no mention of silver causing harm in his *Dracula*. In fact, Jonathan Harker's diary entry of his first encounter with the Count describes the vampire as holding in his hand an antique silver lamp. The first reference I can find in fiction of silver being used against a vampire is, strangely enough, in a Batman comic from 1939. *Detective Comics* issue 32, "Batman vs. The Vampire, Part 2," sees the Caped Crusader encounter the master vampire Monk. Batman kills him with silver bullets (made from melting down candlesticks) fired into his coffin. Monk does claim to have the powers of a werewolf though, so that could be the connection. Much later, in the 1973 film *The Satanic Rites of Dracula*, Professor Van Helsing tries a similar tactic, melting down a silver cross into a single bullet, which he loads into his derringer. Unfortunately, we'll never know if it would have worked, since he misses his one shot. (Dracula eventually dies ridiculously by hawthorn bush.)

For whatever reason, silver started popping up more frequently as a weapon against vampires in the 1990s. In *Vampire$*, the professional slayers in Jack Crow's crew add it to their arsenal in the form of bullets made from holy silver blessed by the Church. However, in this case, silver does not kill, only wounds. In Laurell K. Hamilton's bestselling Anita Blake: Vampire Hunter novels, silver bullets slow vamps down. I'd be tempted to say the trend came as much from the modern obsession with firearms and a desire to get more gunplay into vampire stories as any real interest in the magical powers of silver, but the most interesting use of silver in film and fiction in the 1990s was more creative than that.

Kim Newman's historical horror novel *Anno Dracula* (1992) imagines an alternate ending to Stoker's tale in which Dracula is not killed by Van Helsing and his men but instead goes on to marry Queen Victoria and lead a vampire takeover of the British empire. The book (which was shortlisted for Vampire Novel of the Century by the Horror Writers Association in 2012) mixes characters and events from real life and fiction into a rip-roaring yarn. Set in the era of Jack the Ripper's London crime spree, in this world the vampires are the aristocracy, with different bloodlines having different abilities and weaknesses. The one thing that can kill them all is silver, a kind of poison that counteracts vampires' supernatural regenerative process. (Which is how Dracula escaped Van Helsing's attack in the first place, his wounds simply closed up because the weapons weren't made from silver.) In *Anno Dracula*, metal is difficult to come by though, since the ruling vamps control its production. Still, a backalley silversmith crafts a special sword-cane for Dr. Jack Seward, vampire hunter. You can also procure black market bullets with a lead core and silver exterior that burst in the wound. Bye-bye, bloodsuckers.

If you're still unconvinced that silver should be in your vampire killing kit, consider how well it has served the half-vampire, all-slayer Blade. The comic book character (played by action-movie hero Wesley Snipes in the film trilogy) started using silver to fight vamps when he hit the big screen, big time. Silver stakes. Silver bullets. "Vampire Mace" made from garlic and silver nitrate. Silver garrotte wire. Silver boomerang. And a bad-ass longsword of silver-plated titanium with a impressive providence, having been passed down by vampire slayers through the ages. With all that hand-to-hand combat going on, there doesn't seem to be any time to explain the obsession with silver, but in the final flick, *Blade: Trinity*, we even see colloidal silver sprayed into the ventilation system of a vampire den.

Guillermo del Toro (director of *Blade II*) created a rich mythology for vampires and silver in a trilogy of novels beginning with *The Strain* (2009). In these books (written with Chuck Hogan), vampires, or *strigoi*, are reanimated humans infected with a virus that transforms them into grotesque walking dead with six-foot-long stingers that they use to drink blood. Sunlight is deadly, as is severing their spines or beheading them. But their blood spray is particularly nasty to humans, laden with infectious white worm parasites. And so close combat is always a last resort. Enter silver. The elderly vampire slayer Abraham Setrakian carries a silver sword and is known to decapitate his monsters, chanting the prayer, "*Strigoi*, my sword sings of silver." He explains that silver is "renowned throughout the ages for its antiseptic and germicidal properties," and that while swords of steel or lead can cut vampires, only silver really hurts them.

By the third Strain novel, *The Night Eternal* (2011), vampires have taken over the Earth and silver is outlawed, becoming the "only black-market item worth trafficking in, besides food." And a complex reasoning for its harmfulness to vampires is revealed: vampires are descendents of angels! Way back when, one particular archangel was found biting and drinking from another, and as part of its punishment, it was decreed that silver, the closest substance to angel blood, would forever have an ill effect on vampires.

A different yet equally blibical theory on why vampires might hate silver is presented in Wes Craven's *Dracula 2000* (2000). The horror/action/martial arts flick finds Dracula alive (and sort of well) in the 21st century. A rich antiques dealer calling himself Matthew Van Helsing—grandson of the famous vampire slayer, and played by Christopher Plummer—just happens to be keeping the Count immobilized in a silver coffin in his vault. There is a lot of fighting and a crossbow that shoots silver at some point. But the really interesting part is the big reveal that Dracula is actually none other than Judas, as in Iscariot. He's Vampire Zero, the original undead bloodsucker. Since Judas committed suicide out of guilt for betraying Jesus in exchange for 30 pieces of silver, Dracula simply cannot stand the stuff and is vulnerable in its presence. In the end he dies from exposure to sunlight, but not before giving us one of the most outrageous Dracula backstories ever.

As out there as the Judas theory is, it cropped up again in *Abraham Lincoln: Vampire Hunter* (2012), a big-budget block-buster film based on the 2010 book by Seth Grahame-Smith. As the title suggests, it's an alternate history where Lincoln, before becoming U.S. president, is a vampire slayer. And his weapon of choice is a silver axe. He's told by his mentor that, because of Judas, silver became a "curse upon the cursed," and is thus one of the vampire's weaknesses. At one point, Lincoln (Benjamin Walker) orders the confiscation of the nation's silverware to melt down into weapons against the undead. The film is ridiculously action-packed, with a galloping CGI horse chase, vampires at the battle of Gettysburg, and so on. And in the end, Lincoln kills the master vampire by wrapping his silver pocket watch around his wrist then punching through the monster's chest. Since the film took in more than $116 million, we can be fairly certain that we've not heard the last of this silver-wielding, vampire slaying action hero.

Vampires are allergic to silver in the Southern Vampire Mysteries novels by Charlaine Harris. In the opening scene of the very first novel, *Dead Until Dark* (2001), Sookie, a telepathic waitress in Bon Temps, Louisiana, saves the vampire Bill Compton from a pair of nefarious types who have chained him up in silver, which burns his skin and weakens his powers. Throughout the series, silver chains are used to bind vampires—to restrain them, to torture them, to keep them from feeding—either by humans looking to drain vampires of blood to sell on the black market or by their fellow undead as punishments for crimes.

Vamps can heal from their wounds once the silver is removed, but in season two of the TV show a suicide bomber from an anti-vamp cult, the Fellowship of the Sun, causes fatalities with a silver explosive. In season four, some vampires willingly bind themselves with silver so they won't be able to walk out into the sun after a witch casts a spell that would have them do so. And in season five, silver takes centre stage in several plot lines: a silver IV drip is used to torture prisoners; Bill kills an older, stronger vamp by tricking her into drinking silver-laced blood and then staking her when she is weakened; the vampire Pam uses it like Mace and sprays it in Bill's face, temporarily blinding him; and the old Judas myth appears in a special "holy stake" allegedly tipped with the 30 pieces of silver that belonged to Judas. There's even a shop in Bon Temps, the Stake House, where wannabe slayers can stock up on silver bullets, crossbows, spray and such. Or you can take Pam's advice and pick up some colloidal silver, "in-stock and overpriced at your neighbourhood health food store."

Now that you're convinced that silver can be used to kill vamps, here's a curveball: so can gold. In the 2010 western/horror comic book series *American Vampire* written by Scott Snyder, we encounter Skinner Sweet, an outlaw vampire for a new age. Snyder has explained that he wanted to invent wholly original vamps with new powers and weaknesses. And so there are different species, such as the Carpathians, or the Strigus Gaelic-Prime, all hunted by a group called the Vassals of the Morning Star. For

Sweet and his particular ilk, sunlight doesn't hurt them, wood neither. It's pure gold—gold stakes, gold bullets, etc.—they have to watch out for. Why? Well, according to Sweet, "sometimes when the blood hits someone new, from somewhere new . . . it makes something new. With a whole new bag of tricks." Or more simply: "I'm talking about evolution."

Whether killing vampires with stakes, silver, sunlight or any other material object makes sense to you now or not, it's exciting that writers continue to work hard to come up with fresh tactics to torture their bloodsuckers in books, on television and in movies, digging back through folklore and even the Bible for ideas. Who knows where they will go next? May I humbly suggest they turn the page for my own take on the ultimate weapon.

VI. LOVE

"I've crossed oceans of time to find you."
—Dracula, *Bram Stoker's Dracula*

When Edward Cullen, the dreamy vampire star of the Twilight Saga books and movies, tells his human paramour, Bella Swan, that she is the only thing that can hurt him, he doesn't mean she's a slayer. He means he's in love.

Roll your eyes if you like, but love is a serious threat to all vampires who seek to walk in the shadows, undiscovered by human society, unfettered by ties to mortal life. It causes recklessness and irrationality in all of us, after all, so it's no surprise it also leads to the downfall of many an otherwise indestructible creature. Then there are the living characters in these sagas, those who charge blindly into battle with forces of supernatural evil in order to save their beloveds from death or eternal damnation. Time and time again, love kills.

Love isn't just a concern for the kind of emo vampire populating the young adult and paranormal romance scene of recent years either. In fact, the very first vampire fiction published in English, John Polidori's "The Vampyre," way back in 1819, was originally billed as "a romance of exciting interest." Sure, the villain of that tale, Lord Ruthven, did not perish for his love of the young ladies he bled, but the author did admit to having been influenced by folkloric accounts from Greece of how the vampire is specifically doomed to feed on the ones he loved most in life, a kind of punishment as devastating as any Hell for the living and undead alike.

Appetite for Self-Destruction

Sometimes vampires don't need our help: they bring destruction upon themselves, either deliberately or inadvertently. Here's a sample of some unusual ways vampires can meet true death at their own hands.

Drinking problems

The blood is not always the life. In Anne Rice's *Interview with the Vampire*, Louis is instructed not to drink to the point of the victim's death when feeding. Despite the orgasmic sensation, it would suck the vampire into death. "I would like to think that it would be like that to drink after the victim died, to just glide out of existence, to go out with the tide, it would be like being seduced by death," explained Rice in an interview. In the 1974 comedy/horror film *Blood for Dracula* (a.k.a. *Andy Warhol's Dracula*), a sick and dying Dracula (Udo Kier) travels from Transylvania to Italy because he must drink virgin's blood or he "will be dead in a few weeks." (He thinks a Catholic country will have more virgins.) After feeding from a virgin who's not so virginal after all, he turns green and throws up.

Running with werewolves

In the Underworld series, vamps and werewolves are enemies. Ditto *Twilight*. Just as well. According to *The Vampire Diaries* TV series, a werewolf bite is fatal to vampires. In *Being Human*, werewolf blood burns vampire skin on contact, is poisonous and quick to kill if ingested. In *Van Helsing*, only a werewolf can kill Dracula.

Drowning in it

In some folklore stories, vampires cannot cross running water, apparently because it's associated with purification and washing away sin. But modern vampires seem to have forgotten. In the Hammer film *Dracula: Prince of Darkness* (1966), a priest catches Dracula (Christopher Lee) standing on a frozen river. The priest shoots through the ice and the Count slips under and dies. In *Dracula A.D. 1972* bloodsucker Johnny Alucard (Christopher Neame) falls into bathtub, accidentally turning on the shower, which kills him.

Mommy's dearest

Why aren't there more baby bloodsuckers born into the vampire universe? Maybe because they cannot be trusted. In the novel *Lost Souls* by Poppy Z. Brite, a half-vampire child is rumoured to "eat its way out" of the womb, killing the vampire mother. It took the motherlode of all modern vampire stories, Stephenie Meyer's Twilight Saga, to drive this point home: in *Breaking Dawn*, human Bella gets pregnant from honeymoon sex with vampire Edward. The hybrid fetus begins ripping her apart from the inside: breaking her bones with its kicking, demanding human blood for snacktime. And to actually give birth? Let's just say it's not your ordinary C-section. Some say Meyer's books are just a big ad for teenage abstinence. Yup, that bit oughta do it.

When most vampires in folklore (almost always men) come back from the grave they revisit their women and children first. It seems that even when the entire world (or, at least, as far as you can walk between dusk and dawn) is yours to haunt and hunt, home is still where the heart is. And so old-school vampires are motivated as much by love as bloodlust. (Perhaps if they had chosen to wander further afield for their nightly foraging, they would not have been recognized and could have enjoyed longer undeaths, but then they wouldn't get to hang around their beloveds' bedrooms.) And those family, friends and neighbours who dug up graves and drove wooden stakes into corpses and cut off heads and burned bodies did so not only to protect themselves from vampire influence and attacks but so that their loved ones could be free of the torment of vampirism, to be at peace.

We see this in Bram Stoker's *Dracula*. Professor Van Helsing convinces the three suitors of Lucy Westenra to commit unspeakable acts against her undead body, not so much because she's walking around kidnapping babies but because she is damned and they can't bear the thought of it. After giving a speech about why they need to exhume, stake and decapitate Lucy to prevent her from feeding on others for all of eternity, Van Helsing makes his final pitch: "But the most blessed of all, when this now undead be made to rest as true dead, then the soul of the poor lady whom we love shall again be free." It isn't easy, but from their efforts comes peace for Lucy. Plus, there's one less baby-eating vampire on the prowl.

There is indeed so much breathy romance throughout *Dracula*—the passion between Jonathan Harker and Mina Murray, and everyone else and Lucy—it's no surprise that someone would eventually turn it into a love story. In the 1973 made-for-TV *Bram Stoker's Dracula*, written by *I Am Legend* author Richard Matheson and directed and produced by Dan Curtis (of supernatural soap opera *Dark Shadows* fame), we see for the first time the concept that Dracula is pining for a lost love from centuries past. When Jonathan (Murray

Brown) visits the Count (Jack Palance), he notices a family portrait on the wall with a familiar face in it: a woman bearing a strong resemblance to Lucy (Fiona Lewis), the best friend of his fiancée Mina (Penelope Horner). For his part, the Count sees Jonathan's photo of the two young ladies and decides that Lucy is, in fact, a reincarnation of his love. And so his motivation for travelling from Transylvania to England becomes as much a hunt to woo Lucy as anything else. While he does manage to bite and turn her, which is faithful to Stoker's novel, he also considers her his new bride, and when he finds Lucy staked in her coffin, truly dead, he flies into a rage. You've got to hand it to the man though, he does rebound rather quickly, turning his attention to Mina. Not only does he bite her, he forces her to drink from a cut in his chest, creating a psychic link between them. We know from the book that this link will be his undoing, allowing Professor Van Helsing and his team to track the master vampire and, ultimately, destroy him.

The reincarnated-love angle had been previously concocted by Dan Curtis in his *Dark Shadows* soap and the 1970 film *House of Dark Shadows*. It was also used in the film *Blacula* (1972), in which an African prince-turned-vampire pursues a woman he believes is his wife from 200 years ago. But it was Francis Ford Coppola's production of *Bram Stoker's Dracula* that gave the plot twist unforgettable high production values, imprinting the idea on a new generation.

It's been duly noted by many how this film's title is rather misleading, as two of its key plot elements do not come from Stoker's book at all. Coppola has taken questionable liberty by picking up on the flawed theory that Count Dracula was inspired by the vicious 15th century

Transylvanian prince Vlad "The Impaler" Tepes and making them one and the same. And he's also made Vlad/Dracula and Mina lovers from across "oceans of time" who go on dates to the movies. Ultimately, Mina rejects her handsome prince's affections to run away and marry Jonathan (Keanu Reeves). (Is there anything sadder than the world's greatest vampire breaking down crying reading a Dear John letter?) Then, once again, she uses her psychic link with Vlad/Drac to help Van Helsing (Anthony Hopkins) and his men hunt him down. But true love prevails. In the final destruction scene, Mina rushes to the side of her prince, who has been stabbed with a sword through the heart. Over his body, bloody and grotesquely desiccated, she kisses him and whispers, "My love." And when he gives her the sign that he's had enough, she puts an end to it all by yanking out the sword and using it to slice his head off. And so concludes his reign of terror. Sure, Mina muses how her love has released her and her friends "from the powers of darkness," but it was really Dracula who sacrificed himself, who decided to give up the fight because he could not be with the woman of his dreams. What centuries of warriors couldn't kill, what Van Helsing couldn't defeat, taken down by the beauty of Winona.

It's madness really. But that's love. And, increasingly, it's what makes a vampire a great monster. His flesh may be ice cold, his heart no longer beating, but he can still feel. Remember 1922's *Nosferatu*, and how the horrible Count Orlok is lured to his demise by a woman. Think of the powerful connection between Louis and Lestat in Anne Rice's *Interview with the Vampire*. The bizarre love triangle between slayer Buffy Summers and the vampires

Spike and Angel, the latter of whom gives up his soul for a moment of pure happiness with his teenaged sweetheart. Bill Compton does some pretty stupid shit in the name of his love for Sookie Stackhouse too. It's no coincidence that these are some of the most memorable and beloved vampire tales ever.

So by the time we get to Stephenie Meyer and her beyond-bestselling *Twilight* book in 2005, there shouldn't be anything shocking about vampires in love. The afore-mentioned Edward and Bella are the Romeo and Juliet of their era, as doomed as they are devoted. (I find their relationship to be creepy, abusive and dysfunctional, but that's another book!) Through the four novels in the Twilight Saga and the five films they've spawned, we see how Edward's love for Bella is the chink in his sparkling vampire armour, and how he risks himself and others in pursuit of her safety.

In Meyer's universe, there's only one golden rule: don't expose the secret of vampire existence to humans. The mere fact that Edward confirms his vampire status to Bella without killing or turning her is a bad idea. His "family" is remarkably accommodating of this dalliance, for the sake of his happiness. But when other vamps get the scent of the tasty human in their midst, a cycle of conflict and revenge is set in motion that has serious ramifications for everyone. And still the Cullen clan is determined to protect Bella at all cost. In *New Moon*, Edward breaks things off and leaves town—for her sake, not his. And when he believes her to be dead, he immediately decides to commit suicide. Thing is, for all their prettiness, Twilight vampires are not easily destroyed. Only ripping their bodies apart and burning the pieces will do it. Not easily self-inflicted. So Edward concocts a plan to expose himself to the public in the presence of a ruling clan of vampires, the Volturi, who would certainly execute him for the crime. And so here we have a 104-year-old vampire, gorgeous, powerful and with his whole immortal life ahead of him, throwing everything away over a girl he's (relatively) just met. If you were a slayer looking to destroy him, you couldn't have invented a better weapon.

Another way in which love has destroyed vampires is by making them way less frightening. While millions of readers swoon over Edward Cullen, or the dreamboats of *The Vampire Diaries* and the undead hunks of countless other supernatural romance paperbacks, it has drastically altered the image of the vampire in 21st century popular culture. Horror fans wonder what happened to vicious, bloodsucking monsters. And make no mistake, they are monsters. Monsters who can feel love and passion, sure. Monsters who make fine prom dates, okay. But they are still predators. It's how they survive, by draining humans of blood. It's how they thrive, by doing unspeakable things to innocent people in the night. It's how they've become one of the most enduring legends, enrapturing us with a mix of horror and gore, seduction and lust and fangs, as well as actual mad love. And so whether it's a man fighting to save the woman he loves from a vampire's evil clutches, or a male vampire sacrificing himself for the love of a human woman, there always has to be more to the story than just the romance. There has to be terror. There has to be blood. Otherwise, more than staking, more than decapitation, more than fire or even sunlight, this will be their undoing, the true death for a myth that has crossed, yes, oceans of time. And as much as I do wish my favourite creatures of the night the opportunity to experience love after death, and as much as I support their right to die of heartbreak, I don't want them all to die off forever. And so I beseech those of you writing vampire stories today, use the weapon of love sparingly, with utmost caution. It's the most dangerous of all.

Sacred and Deadly

We've seen how religious objects can ward off a vampire attack or weaken their powers, in folklore as well as fiction. In the right writer's hand, these weapons can also be fatal. Here then, six memorable kill scenes brought to you by the Father, the Son and the Holy Spirit.

Dracula Has Risen from the Grave (1968)
In this Hammer film adaptation of Bram Stoker's novel, the power of prayer is paramount. First, Dracula is prevented from entering his castle after a visiting clergyman affixes a large metal cross to his door. He is later staked by the fiancé of one of his victims, but because the guy is an atheist, it has no effect—Dracula is able to pull out the stake and escape. Ultimately, he falls and is impaled on a cross. While a priest recites a prayer over his struggling, bloody body, the vampire turns to dust.

Captain Kronos – Vampire Hunter (1974)
This rather original Hammer production was a pilot for a British TV series that, sadly, never materialized. Professional slayer Captain Kronos (Horst Janson) and his hunchbacked assistant Professor Hieronymous Grost (John Cater) are called to a village to assist Dr. Marcus (John Carson) in

his investigations into an unusual case of vampirism. When Marcus is bitten and starts to turn, he asks to be killed—for mercy but also to sacrifice himself to research. After several unsuccessful attempts to destroy him (wooden stake, hanging, etc.), Kronos accidently discovers what will kill him: a crucifix. The slayers then get the idea to steal a cross from a cemetery and forge the metal into a holy sword, which they use successfully against the head vampire in a dramatic finale.

They Thirst (1981)

In Robert R. McCammon's epic novel, Father Ramon Silvera goes up against a horde of vampires trying to take over Los Angeles. He wields a crucifix like a sword against one bloodsucker's neck, slicing again and again into the "sizzling wound" until finally the head rips from his body. He then drives the crucifix through the vampire's spine, pinning it to the floor. And in the best use of holy water ever, the vamps are eventually wiped out by massive flooding—which a priest explains killed the creatures because the ocean's salt water is considered blessed and sacred.

The Lost Boys (1987)

This teen vampire film, featuring the newbie slaying team the Frog Brothers, uses every known tactic against a gang of undead during its big battle sequence. One vamp laughs off their efforts to kill him with a bathtub filled with water and garlic bulbs. "Ha ha! Garlic don't work, boys!" he sneers. But Edgar Frog has a comeback as he pushes him into the tub: "Try the holy water, death breath!" And with the hiss of burning skin and the shriek of screams, the vampire goes down for good.

From Dusk till Dawn (1996)

There is rooting and shooting aplenty in this grindhouse gorefest, climaxing with a strip club/barroom brawl against bloodsucking bikers who just can't seem to stay dead. The rag-tag slayers—two gangster brothers, a disenchanted preacher and his kids—brainstorm what they know about vampires and decide their best chance for survival is for the preacher to regain his faith and go on the offensive. "A servant of God can take a cross and shove it up these motherfuckers' asses," I believe was the motivational speech that did it. And so Father Fuller (Harvey Keitel) fashions a "cross" weapon from a shotgun and a baseball bat, holding back the attackers until he can bless all the water for use in condom balloons and his kid's Super Soaker. Hey, maybe the Church will reconsider that stance on condoms now.

Van Helsing (2004)

In this blockbuster action flick, our hero Van Helsing (Hugh Jackman) isn't having much luck using his crossbow in a fight against Dracula's three brides, who are attacking from overhead like harpies. Until his arrows are dripped in holy water—then they become supernaturally, supremely fatal. The fact that the slayer is in the employ of the Vatican surely didn't hurt either.

CHAPTER FOUR

IN PRAISE OF THE SLAYER

As long as there have been legends of vampires, there have been stories of those who've made it their personal quest to destroy them. Some are destined for this duty, others thrust into the job by circumstance. Once upon a time, they were mostly learned, scholarly types, armed with knowledge from dusty books. Today, many prefer to use modern weapons, martial arts training or even magic.

In most traditional folkloric accounts, there were, if not dedicated vampire hunters, at least experts to be called upon to take care of a suspected revenant. Family members of the deceased or other concerned townsfolk would complain to the local religious or government official, who could either investigate themselves or bring in an expert from out of town, such as a medical examiner or representative of the Crown. Legally, anyone could grab a wooden stake, dig up the body and attack the corpse, but it was usually a more formal procedure, and best left to a professional. And in some areas, there were specific people entrusted to the task, ones with unique skills to detect and destroy: vampire slayers.

In ancient Greece, particularly in the north of the country, as well as the neighbouring kingdom of Macedonia, they had the Sabbatarians. These people, born on Saturdays, were considered to have the ability to see ghosts and have a special influence over vampires, which they call *vrykolakas*. According to G.F. Abbott's 1903 publication *Macedonian Folklore*, one Sabbatarian reported luring a vampire into a barn and forcing him to count grain, which distracted the creature long enough that he was able to nail it to a wall. Some Sabbatarians are known to work with a dog, which also has the power to drive away the *vrykolakas*, and Sabbatarian twins apparently could repel vampires just by wearing their clothing inside out (?!). No record seems to have survived on what such men charged for their services, though Abbott takes a swipe at certain "quack" dervishes who operated "ostentatiously," so it seems that con men were not unheard of.

One wonders what it might have cost to hire a *vampirdzhija* in Bulgaria. This Baltic country, bordering Greece and Romania, has one of the most unusual and elaborate ways of eliminating its bloodsuckers, called bottling, along with professionals designated to the task. The *vampirdzhija* (literally "vampire killer") lies in wait for the undead, packing some kind of religious icon such as a painting or other image of Jesus or a holy relic, which he uses to force the creature towards a bottle, inside of which is its favourite food. (No, not blood; Bulgarian vampires actually prefer other food, including manure.) The silly vampire falls for the snack trap and bang!—the *vampirdzhija* captures it in the bottle then whisks it away to be burned. Cheque, please!

These traditional European vampire slayers were almost like sorcerers, using secret skills and mysterious rituals to cleanse their communities of evil. For most of the 20th century, fictional vampire slayers of the page and screen became more like arms of the law, bounty hunters or rogue soldiers, chivalrous heroes out to save a damsel from sanguinary distress using weapons training and bravado. But things have since shifted yet again. While modern slayers (which now include women as well as men) may take their cues from folklore (stakes, for example, are still essentially standard issue), their creators have gifted them with original abilities and compelling backstories of their own to make them just as, if not more, popular than the villains they set out to fight. It's part of the current trend to write vampires into complex supernatural universes, as exemplified by such successful book and TV series as *Buffy the Vampire Slayer*, *True Blood* and *The Vampire Diaries*, where conflicts extend well beyond human versus vamps. Slayers are now expected to deal also with werewolves, fairies, witches, shape-shifters, demons and all manner of supernatural evils, requiring far more weaponry than mere holy water and crucifixes. As such, many new vampire hunters have reverted back to traditional tactics, particularly magical abilities or knowledge.

Unfortunately, despite the ever-expanding job description, the slayer may soon be out of work. As more and more vampire stories are told from the point of view of the undead, or those who love them, emphasis on the powers and influence of the solitary slayer has started to wane. Instead we now read about entire vampire societies with clans, kingdoms and infighting (vamps in *True Blood* and the Anita Blake books are awfully territorial) and more institutionalized or centuries-old enemies, such as the werewolves in Twilight or Underworld. (I suspect the influence of role-playing games, notably *Vampire: The Masquerade*, in developing a taste for these types of epic battles.) In recognition of all they've done in the past to keep vampires dead but vampire lore alive, and in the hopes they'll still be around to battle tomorrow's nocturnal nasties, here profiled are some of the most enduring literary and cinematic slayers.

I. Professor Abraham Van Helsing, MD, PhD, DLitt

"We have on our side power of combination — a power denied
to the vampire kind; we have resources of science; we are
free to act and think; and the hours of the day and night are
ours equally. We have self-devotion to a cause, and an end to
achieve which is not a selfish one. These things are much."

Professor Van Helsing is a Dutch medical doctor and a
scholar created by Irish author Bram Stoker as the hero/
expert for his gothic horror novel *Dracula*. Stoker's research
notes indicate the character may have been named after
Bram (short for Abraham) and/or his father (also an
Abraham). Stoker wanted his story to have a scholar,
a researcher and a detective. In Van Helsing, Stoker
wrapped all of those things into one complex, contradictory man, one with faith in both superstition and science.
He is one of the only characters in *Dracula* who is described
physically. The character Mina Murray writes in her diary
that he's "a man of medium height, strongly built, with his
shoulders set back over a broad, deep chest. . . . The face,
clean-shaven, shows a hard, square chin, a large, resolute
mobile mouth, a good-sized nose . . . big, bushy eyebrows
. . . reddish hair, big, dark blue eyes." He is described as
carrying with him a leather bag in which he keep a lantern,
wax candles, soldering iron, oil lamp, surgical knives,

sacred consecrated wafers and, most importantly, a three-foot-long wooden stake and heavy hammer.

The Professor is the main source of information about vampires in *Dracula*; although he is at first reticent to alarm others with his suspicions, ultimately he delivers a passionate lecture on the legend of the creatures and just how to go about killing one: "Wild rose on his coffin keep him that he move not from it . . . a sacred bullet fired into the coffin kill him so he be true dead, a stake through him and cutting off the head giveth rest." In this scene, Van Helsing demonstrates the true value of the fictional vampire hunter, outlining the rules of his particular story's monster for both the other characters and the reader. It's a bit of necessary exposition that is repeated in almost every vampire story to follow, as cliché as the big reveal of the murderer in a mystery. And so it doesn't matter that Van Helsing isn't the one who kills Dracula in the end. He is still an essential part of his destruction.

The character was first brought to life on the stage by American actor Edward Van Sloan, who was then cast as a very respectable, bespectacled Van Helsing in the classic Universal Pictures version, as well as the sequel *Dracula's Daughter*. But it's Englishman Peter Cushing that most embodied Van Helsing in his five films as the character for Hammer. In the classic *Horror of Dracula*, he brought new athleticism and action to the role, particularly in the dramatic final fight with Christopher Lee's Dracula, which was copied by other cinematic slayers and became a trope of the vampire film genre. It's no wonder Hammer brought Cushing back, even when Dracula wasn't in the film (1960's *Brides of Dracula*) or after Van Helsing had died. (He had showdowns with Lee as a descendant of the professor in *The Satanic Rites of Dracula*.) Not only was Peter Cushing the most famous Van Helsing, he was the actor most associated with the figure of the vampire slayer until Sarah Michelle Gellar's Buffy Summers came along in the late '90s.

As a book character, Van Helsing has proven to be as popular and adaptable as Dracula himself. In the 1975 novel *The Dracula Tape* by Fred Saberhagen the roles are reversed and he's the villain to the Count's hero. (This is one of the first books to portray the vampire in a positive light.) The 2004 short story anthology *The Many Faces of Van Helsing* features, amongst many wonderfully original works, the wicked tale "The Screaming" by J.A. Konrath, in which Van Helsing is himself a vampire, being kept chained in a basement, starving and begging to die. If only he could have cloned and hired himself to end his own misery.

On film, Van Helsing has been portrayed with great flourish by such prominent actors as Laurence Olivier (1979's *Dracula*), Anthony Hopkins (*Bram Stoker's Dracula*) and Christopher Plummer (*Dracula 2000*), as well by countless forgettable faces in unmentionable B movies. In 2004, he got top billing in the action movie *Van Helsing*, the Hollywood "tribute" to classic monsters, which reimagined him as Gabriel Van Helsing, an agent of God who was trained by monks and mullahs and now works for the Vatican. His mission is divine: save the Princess Anna Valerious from Dracula because nine generations of her family are trapped in purgatory until they fulfill a promise to destroy the Count. Australian Hugh Jackman plays him as a sassy Indiana Jones–type (weathered hat and all) who packs explosives, silver stakes, crossbows and holy water. Unfortunately, he finds out Dracula cannot be killed by any of these methods, only by a werewolf. Fortunately, he gets bitten by a werewolf and, once transformed, is able to do the deed. (Hey, thank me for the spoiler; now you don't have to see this wretched film.) Surely, this is one of the most memorable vampire slaying tactics in recent memory, as creative as it is ridiculous. Speaking of ridiculous, there's more than a little Van Helsing in *Abraham Lincoln: Vampire Hunter*, the 2010 novel adapted for the big screen in 2012. Van Helsing's transformation from gentleman professor to action hero is thus complete. But the foundations of his character, that relentless pursuit of Dracula and other undead predators armed with scientific knowledge and faith in God, has influenced every other fictional vampire slayer who's come along since.

II. Robert Neville

"If I didn't kill them, sooner or later they'd die and come after me. I have no choice, no choice at all."

Robert Neville was created by American author Richard Matheson for his 1954 book *I Am Legend*, which in 2012 was proclaimed the Bram Stoker Vampire Novel of the Century by the Horror Writers Association. It has had a profound influence on horror storytelling in general; not only does the theme of an entire society of vampires taking over the world start here, much of the plague and siege themes that have dominated zombie movies in the last four decades owe it a great debt. It has been adapted for the screen several times, notably 1964's *The Last Man on Earth* starring Vincent Price as Neville, 1971's *The Omega Man* starring Charlton Heston and 2007's *I Am Legend* starring Will Smith. In the 1990s, it was also turned into a comic book series by Steve Niles and Elman Brown.

In Matheson's original story, Robert Neville is 36 years old and living in Los Angeles. He's lost his wife, Virginia, and daughter, Kelly, to the mysterious plague, and while initially skeptical that the dead were coming back to life, he revises his views after an undead Virginia comes rapping on his door. Neville is uniquely immune to the global pandemic, but these vamps are intent on killing him, forcing him to seek out and destroy them for self-preservation.

He dedicates himself to the puzzle of how this supernatural legend could have a basis in science: if he can determine the actual cause of the plague, he can develop a cure for the vampire "disease" and restore humanity to Earth. His daylight hours are thus spent split between research and scientific experiments in his fortified home and patrols of the desolate city, staking or shooting any bloodsuckers he can find—all the while trying to keep from losing his mind from loneliness.

In a nice nod to the mother of all vampire tales, Neville at one point reads a passage from Bram Stoker's *Dracula*. But the rational scientist quickly dismisses the mythology outlined in the book as mere superstition. He differs from Van Helsing in that he is not an expert at the outset: he must become one, transforming from skeptic to slayer over the course of the story. Like Van Helsing, however, Neville plays both sides: he hangs garlands of garlic on his front door to keep the vamps at bay just in case, but also researches the physical properties of the garlic bulb in the hopes of distilling it into a weapon. He questions the use of crucifixes, which he discovers only work on reanimated Christians of faith, and determines he'll need a Torah for Jewish vampires. Why do some vampires turn immediately to dust when staked, while others simply croak, their corpses left to be disposed of? Why do some succumb to a shot from a pistol, while others keep on shuffling? Robert Neville methodically dissects the legends and conducts various tests until he decides that vampires could have both supernatural and scientific origins. He ultimately fixates on an evil germ that lives on fresh blood, which he dubs "*vampiris.*"

As best portrayed by Vincent Price in *The Last Man on Earth* (even though the character's name was changed to Dr. Robert Morgan for some reason), Neville is a different kind of vampire hunter. He has no special powers. He doesn't train to fight. (The vampires are weak, like zombies, or "animals after a famine," which helps.) His slaying does not involve dramatic chase scenes or action sequences. It's not a passion or a calling. No, for him, vampire hunting is more like a daily chore: carving his own stakes, packing them into his bag along with a mallet, exploring the next block of houses in a grid search, staking vampires in their sleep wherever he can find them, then carting their bodies to a giant pit of fire where they'll be disposed of, never to return. A grisly routine.

The blockbuster remake with Will Smith was, not surprisingly, more Disneyfied, with hulking CGI monsters and SUV chases through an abandoned Manhattan. But as Lieutenant Colonel Robert Neville, a military virologist, Smith maintained the character's scientific obsessions, experimenting on infected rats and the occasional trapped vampire. In the *Omega Man* version, Neville is more of an action hero, fighting with a stash of automatic weapons. But his vampires aren't actually vampires: they're a religious cult (or family) of albino mutants who are light-sensitive and say "brother" a lot. But when their leader, Matthias, gives a speech on how they "were chosen just for this work. To bury what was dead. To bury what was evil. To destroy what was dangerous," it sounds an awful lot like the life of a slayer. And as Robert Neville exemplified, the more vampires there are to face, the lonelier that life can be.

III. Blade

"You're not immortal. I musta heard hundreds of you rodents
make the same claim. Each one of them tasted the end of my
sword." —Blade, *Blade: Trinity*

For 30 years, the half-man, half-vampire, all bad-ass
slayer Blade has been slicing and dicing vamps and other
supernatural creatures in comic books, films, television
and anime, most famously in three action movies where
the character was played by Wesley Snipes. Created by Marv
"Wicked Comic Book Name" Wolfman for Marvel's *Tomb
of Dracula* in 1973, Blade is one of few African-American
superheroes in comics, brought to life to give the ol'
Count some fresh, socially relevant opponents in the age
of Black Power. He soon got his own storylines, which over
the decades have sent him racing around a world overrun
with vampires, fighting Dracula several times, working
for various government agencies and alongside other
Marvel slayers such as Quincy Harker (son of Stoker's
Jonathan) and Rachel Van Helsing (great-granddaughter
of Abraham), and even time-travelling. In the three feature films, Blade reprises some of those great battles as he
fights to save humanity from a complete vampire takeover.

The Hollywood movie Blade differs significantly from
his comic book origins, in both appearance and abilities.
The original character (whose real name is Eric Brooks)

was drawn by artist Gene Colan as a fairly regular guy, one who wore a bandolier stocked with wooden knives over his three-quarter-length trenchcoat, and goggles to keep tainted vampire blood from splashing into his eyes during kills—perhaps a nod to the old practice of covering up the bodies of suspected revenants with cloth or animal hide to prevent any blood spatter during staking. He need not have worried about that thanks to his unusual birth. His pregnant mother was attacked by a bloodsucker in the hospital during his delivery (under a "blood moon" no less). This nasty bit of business ultimately led to her death, while blessing/cursing Blade with a unique physiology and a blinding obsession to kill not only the man responsible but all vampires on Earth. As a *dhampir* he enjoys "all of the strengths and none of the weaknesses" of vamps. Though not truly immortal (he ages very, very slowly and can regenerate from wounds very, very quickly), Blade has immunity from sunlight, and from vampire bites, meaning no stinking revenant saliva was going to transform him into a full-on bloodsucker. And after he is bitten by "The Living Vampire" Morbius, he acquires supernatural abilities: extreme strength and highly developed senses of smell, sight and hearing, which, when combined with years of training in the martial arts, make for a rather lethal combination of slaying skills indeed.

Under different comic book artists in the 1990s, his look evolved too. By the time movie-goers met him in the 1998 film, he'd become a real pre-millennial dark knight: dressed head to toe in black, covered in tribal tattoos, his bulging biceps straining the seams of his imposing (and, let's face it, rather impractical) long black leather coat—lined dramatically in blood red. The goggles have been replaced with cool shades, the hand-carved stakes with a titanium samurai sword he keeps slung over his back.

The upgraded weaponry makes Blade a prime example of how vampire slayers were changing at the end of the 20th century. While 1970s Blade used wooden knives and daggers carved from teak, tools straight out of centuries-old folklore, 1990s movie star Blade packs science and technology: hollow-point, garlic-filled silver bullets. The use of silver as a means of destroying vamps does go back to the comics—Blade first learned to slay from Jamal Afari, a jazz horn-playing, drug-addicted vampire hunter who used a silver cane as a weapon, and, like a kind of monster Mr. Miyagi, trained Blade when he was a child. But for the films, screenwriter David S. Goyer transformed that mentor character into Abraham Whistler (Kris Kristofferson), a grizzled weapons expert with a full-on hate-on for vampires, ever since they slaughtered his wife and daughters. Whistler develops a synthetic serum for Blade to help him control his vampire bloodlust so he doesn't need to drink human plasma. He also supplies the slayer with an arsenal of high-tech gizmos to target his enemies' weaknesses, such as "vampire Mace," a combination of garlic (which sends them into anaphylactic shock) and silver nitrate, or a portable UV lamp, to simulate sunlight. Between the two of them, it's actually Whistler who exhibits the most classic vampire hunter behaviour, tucked away in his workshop researching modern scientific developments to aid in their cause, expertise which Blade and his physical prowess can then put into action.

The 2002 sequel *Blade II* steps up the weaponry several

notches—as well as everything else; what a gorgeous monster movie—as Blade joins a tactical unit of vamps known as the Blood Pack. Originally put together to destroy him, they decide to work together in order to fight off a new mutant strain of vampires called Reapers that threaten to assimilate both human and vampire worlds. These Reapers are nasty: bald, with translucent skin and downright disgusting mouth stingers, they crawl in the subterranean shadows. With much more in common with the old rat-like *nosferatu* than the slick vamps that populate most contemporary vampire cinema, they are a wholly fresh creation of director Guillermo del Toro (similar creatures appeared later in his vampire novel *The Strain*). In the film's DVD commentary, del Toro admits his goal for *Blade II* was to ensure no two fights would be the same, and so we see Blade wielding plenty of new toys such as bullets and syringes filled with EDTA (an anti-coagulant that makes a vampire's head explode), and UV flashbang grenades, while still exhibiting the creative combat and swordplay that defines him. (In the 2011 Marvel Anime series, he wields even more magical martial arts moves including "Residual Moon," "Phantom Moon" and "Chaotic Moon.") In the third film, 2004's *Blade: Trinity*, he once again confronts Dracula (who now calls himself "Drake," for some reason, and looks like he stepped out of an Axe bodyspray ad instead of a crypt, unfortunately), aided by a plucky gang of "Nightstalkers" out to develop an airborne bio-weapon that will destroy all vampires. Amongst their weapons is atomized colloidal silver in a compressed gas projectile, designed to be deployed with

IN PRAISE OF THE SLAYER

a crossbow and ultimately delivered in a hand-to-hand showdown.

What makes Blade Blade is not, well, his blade, or even his half-vampire status. It's his singular purpose: Destroy. All. Vampires. Everywhere. Unlike so many others who are forced or who choose to kill the walking dead, he never suffers from a lack of faith. Even if he has to use innocent people as bait, kill a human servant (a "familiar") or take down a vamp in the body of a former friend, he does it with absolute conviction, to the point of turning down a possible cure for his own vampire curse so that he can continue his mission. He may have started with a personal score to settle, but he goes far beyond that type of vengeance. He's not slaying to save a love interest, a child or even his own soul. Blade walks in the daylight to protect humanity from a scourge, whatever the personal cost—a true action hero for an apocalyptic world.

IV. The Frog Brothers

"Our number is on the back. Pray you never need to call us."
—Alan Frog, *The Lost Boys*

The Frog Brothers are some of the youngest experts in vampire film, starring in the 1987 classic *The Lost Boys*, its sequels *Lost Boys: The Tribe* (2008) and *Lost Boys: The Thirst* (2010), as well as the four-issue comic book series *The Lost Boys: Reign of Frogs* (2008). They were created by screenwriters Janice Fischer and James Jeremias, originally as eight-year-old chubby Cub Scout types for a film about kid vampires inspired by *Peter Pan*. Director Joel Schumacher mercifully transformed that idea into *The Lost Boys*, making the characters older. While not top billed in the original film, the Frog Brothers were so popular with viewers they went on to star in the sequels. (The tag line for *Lost Boys: The Thirst* was "The Frog Brothers are back for blood.")

Edgar (Corey Feldman) and Alan Frog (Jamison Newlander), teen brothers from the "murder capital of the world," Santa Carla, California, work in their parents' comic book shop as a cover for their vampire hunting, although they initially do more reading than slaying. When fellow comic book fan Sam Emerson (Corey Haim) and his family move to town, they attract the attention of the local vamp gang. Edgar and Alan (their names are a salute to Edgar Allan Poe) must spring into action when

Sam's older brother, Michael (Jason Patric) becomes a half-vampire by drinking blood on a dare by the gang. They need to slay Santa Carla's head vampire in order to return him to his normal, human self.

Edgar and Alan possess the core characteristics of old school vampire hunters. They believe in the existence of undead bloodsuckers while those around them do not, they then set about proving it through research, and ultimately they lead the fight against vampires with great conviction—although they may be the first to use horror comic books as their primary reference material. (Upon first meeting Sam in the shop, they press a copy of the comic *Vampires Everywhere* into his hands with the warning, "Take this. It could save your life.")

The Frog Brothers may be book smart, but they lack any formal training. Without any specific skills, supernatural abilities or experience, they are forced to learn on the job. When it's time to prepare for their first actual encounter with vampires, they carve their own wooden stakes, then get on their BMX bikes and go steal holy water from a church. They wear army combat clothing, dog tags and face paint, reflecting their attitude to fight for "truth, justice and the American way."

As supporting characters, the Frog Brothers don't directly destroy the head vampire in *The Lost Boys* or even the gang leader, but they are responsible for several of the film's spectacular kills. After descending into the gang's cavern lair and finding the vampires hanging from the ceiling like bats, Edgar crawls up and drives a stake through the heart of one, unleashing spurts of blood, screams of pain and a rather pissed-off pack. Their youthfulness is played up with sassy age-appropriate dialogue (when a vamp falls back into a sound system and gets electrocuted, the teens gleefully exclaim, "Death by stereo!") and weaponry (squirt guns filled with holy water).

Edgar Frog returned in *Lost Boys: The Tribe*, in which he refers to himself as a "surfboard shaper and vampire hunter." Coming 20 years after the original, and heading straight to DVD, few fans saw the film. Ditto *The Thirst*, where Edgar is older and living in a trailer without many prospects, until a writer of "vampire romance" novels comes looking for help to kill the vamp who kidnapped her brother in Ibiza: a club promoter/drug dealer named DJ X. Yeah, that third film is a time capsule of clichés from the 2000s: ravers, ecstasy, reality TV stars, etc. Alan is there, as a half-vampire working as a taxidermist. Sam is dead though, just like actor Corey Haim. The film features new and improved weaponry (crucifix-shaped stakes, machine guns, UV lamps) and such cornball action movie lines as "Why don't you go suck yourself!" Again, not that anyone saw it.

The Frog Brothers' time in the spotlight was short-lived, but they were important in the widening of the slayer role to include teenagers. As young people leading the charge to save the day, they joined Mark Petrie of 1975's *Salem's Lot* and Charlie Brewster in 1985's *Fright Night* in giving a new generation of monster kids raised on comics their own vampire hunting heroes to root for.

V. Anita Blake

"I am the Executioner. And I don't date vampires, I kill them."
—Anita Blake, *Guilty Pleasures*

Created by writer Laurell K. Hamilton, Anita Blake has appeared in 21 bestselling novels that blend horror and fantasy with crime and romance, beginning with 1993's *Guilty Pleasures* and including such titles as *Burnt Offerings* (1998), *Incubus Dreams* (2004) and *Kiss the Dead* (2012). Hamilton has explained in interviews that her original manuscript was rejected multiple times by publishers who simply didn't know what to do with it: "Mixed genre was a dirty word in publishing, because it didn't sell," she said.

As a professional necromancer and licensed vampire hunter, Anita Blake is not only one of the first female slayers but also one of few who get to do it out in the open. (I hope she keeps receipts for garlic to claim on her taxes.) In a parallel universe where supernatural creatures exist openly and are bound by rule of law, Blake works for Animators Inc., where she raises zombies for hire and assists criminal investigations. Her motivation is like that of most law enforcement types: protect the innocent. To this end, she uses her street smarts, her intimate knowledge of the supernatural community, her black belt skills in judo and a lot of handguns. She kills vampires because it's her job to take down undead criminals, although she often finds herself in unusual situations requiring some quick slaying action. Also, lots of romance and sex action: despite her oft-quoted declaration that she doesn't date vampires, Anita Blake likes to keep her friends close, and her enemies closer.

Clearly, Hamilton was ahead of her time: a monster-slaying heroine with dating problems? Anita Blake preceded the supernatural chick lit phenomenon by about a decade and TV's similarly themed *Buffy the Vampire Slayer* by several years. But despite a Marvel comic adaptation in the late 2000s, and talk of a TV movie or series with IFC (which fell through in 2010), crossover exposure has pretty much eluded Blake. It could be due to Hamilton breaking off from the mainstream pack by shifting from horror/fantasy into erotica.

From the start, Blake was hooking up with the master vampire, but as the series progressed Hamilton plunged her heroine head-on into erotica with something she called "the ardeur"—a powerful force that allows one to feed on lust. It also turns you into a nymphomaniac, apparently, as Anita now spends as much time getting it on with assorted creatures of the night as she does killing them. There's also a "triumvirate" that boosts her abilities when connected to two others, basically a fancy name for a monster ménage à trois.

When she does get down to the business of slaying, Anita Blake packs small concealable weapons such as 9mm handguns or a trusty wooden stake, plus an insubordinate attitude. Like many humans caught in the web of supernatural struggles, she wrestles with her own morality and humanity. Raised Catholic (and practising until the Pope excommunicated all animators at which point she defected to Episcopalian), she carries a Christian faith that serves her very well when brandishing holy water, crucifixes and other sacred objects in the face of vampire threats.

Unfortunately, and despite her training and abilities, Anita Blake finds herself often being the one targeted, at risk, fighting for her own survival instead of society's. In this respect, she exhibits a personal vulnerability not often shown in the slayer, which may have endeared her to a loyal fanbase but has made for a somewhat less than stellar vampire hunter. Though she was a trailblazer for women in the slayer biz and continues to sell a lot of novels for Hamilton, Anita Blake's impact on vampire lore has remained somewhat limited. Certainly when compared to the young woman who came after her.

VI. Buffy Summers

"I would love to be upstairs watching TV or gossiping about boys or, god, even studying! But I have to save the world. Again." —Buffy, "Becoming, Part 2"

Created by screenwriter Joss Whedon for the 1992 film *Buffy the Vampire Slayer* (starring Kristy Swanson), Buffy Summers is one of the strongest slayers ever known. She truly emerged as a force in vampire lore with the 1997 television series of the same name, starring Sarah Michelle Gellar. For seven seasons, the character Whedon has described as "Barbie with a kung-fu grip" messed with the conventions of both the vampire hunter and the horror genre's blonde bimbo. In Sunnydale, California (which is located atop a Hellmouth), vampires and other creatures are kept from taking over the world by the heroic efforts of the Sunnydale High student, the latest "Chosen One" in a worldwide network of predestined young female slayers, one for each generation, serving until death. Buffy thus finds herself at the centre of a secret supernatural struggle she must lead all the while battling the ordinary dramas of adolescent life. A reluctant heroine, Buffy learns to embrace her destiny as guardian of the Hellmouth and ends up fighting off more vamps and other monsters ("baddies," in Buffyspeak) than most other slayers on this list, combined.

She doesn't do this alone. While the other slayers we

meet in the show are fiercely independent, Buffy fights alongside her friends, most notably fellow Sunnydale students Xander Harris (Nicholas Brendon) and Willow Rosenberg (Alyson Hannigan), who dub themselves "The Scooby Gang." Rubert Giles (Anthony Stewart Head), the school's librarian, is Buffy's secret "watcher," a guardian who trains and protects her. Together, Giles, Buffy and her pals are like a modern version of Van Helsing and his enlisted vampire hunting team in the original *Dracula*. But there are major differences between Ms. Summers and those who have gone before her. Whedon creates a slayer mythology, which has its own complex rules and history, revealed gradually throughout the series. We eventually learn that slayers' superhuman strength, speed and accelerated healing come from an ancient group of African shamans (the so-called "Shadow Men") who used magic to insert the soul of a demon into an ordinary girl against her will. And when a Chosen One is activated as a slayer, like Buffy was at age 15, she is gifted with physical enhancements not unlike those of her bloodsucking foes, actually. But that's not quite enough. Under Giles's watch, she trains in martial arts.

One of Buffy's key roles in Sunnydale is to go out on patrols—walking the cemeteries in search of vampires rising from their graves or the streets to find the undead up to no good. In addition, she often uncovers some kind of sinister plot which needs to be resolved, usually by destroying a vampire. Her preferred weapon is a stake, although she's been known to use holy water, axes and crossbows. She is sometimes gifted with special, more magical talismans or weapons, and even an "Emergency Slayer Kit."

Though she isn't afraid to use a rocket launcher in one episode, she's not a gun-toting slayer.

Given the fact that the show produced 144 episodes, there were many storylines large and small, different kinds of monsters and ways to kill them (including some inconsistencies). More than ever, fighting vampires is complicated. Not because Buffy lacks the tools or training but because the bad guys aren't always all bad. In fact, the stories that defined the character the most involved love interests from the vampire realm: Angel and Spike. She lost her virginity at age 17 to Angel, a vampire cursed with a soul. (Until the curse was lifted and she then had to send him to Hell. Naturally.) Spike originally came to Sunnydale to slay the slayer, but then fell in love with her, which turned him from Mr. Bad-Ass to Mr. Bad Romance. These are two vampires Buffy the Vampire Slayer is simply unable to kill. They weave in and out of her life, turning from good to bad and back again, and reminding viewers that as much as Buffy has a mission of universal consequence, the show is also about real-life problems that can seem very much like the end of the world, especially to a high school girl. You know, like boys.

Where Buffy truly kicks ass is in the TV show's final season, when she calls upon all of the "potential slayers"— teenage girls in line to become the next slayer when she dies (for the third time). Giles brings them to Sunnydale to protect them, but Buffy trains them to fight. Not later— now. This twist, this refusal to stand by and wait for a system devised by some old patriarchal council to kick in, proves once again that Buffy is an ordinary girl of extraordinary powers. Using magic and a mystical scythe, Buffy, a gang of newly activated potentials and the Scoobies take on the Turok-Han (the oldest, and ugliest, vamps) and the First Evil. Screw prophecy, let's kill some vampires.

Much has been written, by pop culture critics, academics, sociologists and even philosophers, on the layers of meaning in *Buffy*. It's a genre program of an epic nature, with its intricate doomsday scenarios (which continued to play out in comic books after the apocalyptic TV finale) that challenged what a vampire story about teenagers could be. And if at times all the meaning can distract from the fact that Buffy Summers is at heart just a really bitchin' vampire hunter the likes of which we'd never yet seen, well, in her own words, remember that she is simply, definitively the Chosen One. "Ask around. Look it up: 'Slayer, comma the.'"

The Vampire Dispatch Kit

In June 2010, esteemed British auction house Christie's put this item up for bid: "Vampire Killing Kit. One 19th century box with later additions, containing crucifix and four stakes, Bible from 1873, European pocket pistol, iron-mounted shot flask, bullet mould, syringe, photograph of a priest, four vials and another crucifix, all of various dates from the nineteenth to late twentieth centuries." Estimated value? Between $2,000 and $3,000 USD. Actual selling price? $8,712. Not to be outdone, in April 2012, Sotheby's listed its own kit. It sold for $13,750—over $10,000 more than anticipated. Pretty cool.

The vampire killing kit offers everything a wannabe slayer could want: wooden stakes, a crucifix, holy water, garlic or rosary beads and sometimes a firearm loaded with silver bullets, all in a pretty velvet-lined box. Produced in the late 1800s at the height of the vampire hysteria, they were sold to travellers visiting eastern Europe to protect them against any encounters with the undead. For today's vampire fan and collector, the high-end item is a kind of Holy Grail acquisition. They are beautiful, historical and, of course, handy for slaying vampires. Only one problem: it's a hoax.

If you read the auction description carefully, you'll notice it specifies "later additions." That's because the vampire killing kit as a 19th century artefact never existed. Oh, the boxes are generally quite old. And some of the contents can be too. But the chances the kits themselves were made during Bram Stoker's lifetime? Unlikely indeed.

After a series of high-profile auctions and the subsequent media attention, antique firearm experts started poking around the providence of these kits. What they discovered is that the kits are assembled in modern times from old objects, then made to look as if the whole thing was crafted a century or more ago. Someone even went to the trouble of creating a fake manufacturer, "Ernst Bloomberg," and attaching his label to the boxes; these so-called Bloomberg kits are now considered the most authentic, even though there was no Bloomberg. The fact is that they are modern novelty items, probably no older than the 1970s, made to cash in on the current vampire craze, not the original one.

The vampire killing kit still makes a gorgeous gift for the vampire lover in your life. You can often find them listed for auction on eBay or other sites but those usually sell for inflated prices due to their alleged "antique" nature. Better to buy a new one handmade for you by an independent craftsperson. You can also see a "real" "antique" vampire killing kit on display at a Ripley's Believe It or Not museum. Just don't believe the hype.

CHAPTER FIVE

A FEW WORDS ON VAMPIRE SUICIDE

> "The passing years will drive you to madness. To see others
> grow old and die, to see kingdoms rise and fall, to lose all you
> understand and cherish—who can endure it?"
> —Magnus, *The Vampire Lestat*

Vampires aren't supposed to live forever.

I realize in writing that, it will confuse a lot of readers who equate vampires with immortality. But the two weren't always synonymous. If you think of the origin of the legend, vampires were merely revenants. Their destiny was to be tracked down and put out of their misery, by rather gruesome means of impalement and dismemberment, I may add. To be released into the peace of "true death" so that the living could go on, uninterrupted by the hauntings and disease that were the hallmarks of such a creature's arrival in their midst. The vampire existed to help the living deal with the mysteries of sudden death. It was not meant to be a fantasy, a model for some alternative lifestyle where you get seduced by a gorgeous stranger then transformed into a super-powerful being that never ages, never dies.

Yes, vampires have evolved. And those of us who are fascinated by them are the better for it. Oh, the places we've seen, through their eyes. The love stories we've been drawn into, the epic battles we've felt like we were taking part in. As immortals living out multiple lives over centuries, vampires have been our guides through history, into other civilizations and societies, and sometimes even the future. But while we have been enraptured and entertained, they have suffered.

In the seminal vampire tale *Varney the Vampyre*, lead villain Sir Francis Varney is full of self-loathing for his nature. He's terrible at being a vampire, for a start—his nighttime feasting on the necks of maidens is usually interrupted by some family member or servant, and he's constantly on the run from angry, stake-wielding mobs. His supernatural strengths and ability to regenerate from injuries by the light of the full moon don't delight or satisfy him. He sees himself not as gifted, but cursed. This kind of brooding bloodsucker was a departure from the terrifying beast of folklore and a precursor for Lestat and Angel and Edward and all the other beautiful vampires who just don't know what to do with all of that beauty. And what did Varney do about his angst, eventually? He killed himself by jumping into a volcano. He became fiction's first vampire suicide.

Despair is not something Bram Stoker really addresses in *Dracula*, since his book is written from everyone's point of view except for the Count's. Who knows what inner turmoil he was battling, and what fate he might have chosen for himself if allowed to escape from Van Helsing's clutches. But as vampires became more complex—more human—in the 20th century, so did their troubles, and by the time we get to Anne Rice's Vampire Chronicles in the 1970s, it's firmly established that these creatures of the night are immortal, and that's not all it's cracked up to be.

In fact, Rice's whole saga begins with misery and hopelessness. The narrator of *Interview with the Vampire*, Louis de Pointe du Lac, outlines his history: as a young man he was suicidal, overcome with grief and guilt over the death of his brother. Bent on self-destruction, he wandered seedy New Orleans looking for danger and death. He found instead the "dark gift" of the vampire Lestat, who transformed him into a vampire, a vampire too sensitive to kill and so desperate to uncover the mysteries of the undead universe that he could barely get by on its simple pleasures—like unlimited buxom women and luxurious accommodations. Were he to have known Lestat's origin story, or the fate of several of his "ancestors," he would surely have not been any happier.

Rice's universe is filled with vampires struggling to deal with their eternal life. Many literally go underground for centuries, taking a break from watching the world go by as they stay the same. For those who don't, madness awaits. As the chronicles unfold over several novels, we witness suicide on a pretty regular basis. It especially seems to surround Lestat. We learn how Lestat's maker, Magnus, killed himself by jumping into fire almost immediately after siring the young vamp. We see his friend and lover Nicolas de Lenfent go insane, and eventually he demands to be set ablaze on a funeral pyre. Lestat himself, lonely and depressed, goes walking out into the sun.

Fatal exposure to sunlight seems to be the way to go for most vampires facing depression and disillusionment. It's the one thing they can easily access and that requires no accomplice. It's also a glorious denouement for a movie.

In the comic book and film *30 Days of Night*, Eben doesn't want to be a vampire. But he voluntarily turns himself into one in order to acquire the supernatural strength that will allow him to fight off the undead that have been slaughtering his town. After the final battle, he joins his ex-wife to watch the sun come up; the two embracing until the end as his body turns into ashes. For Eben, life as one of the bloodthirsty monsters is not an option—with suicide his sacrifice is complete. *Blade II* has a similarly poetic ending. The beautiful vampire Nyssa (Leonor Varela) is attacked and bitten by a vicious "Reaper" super vamp. She tells Blade her last wish is to see a sunrise, and to die as a vampire rather than transform into a Reaper. Ever the hero, Blade carries her out to meet the dawn, and when the sun rises she disintegrates to ashes in his arms. In both of these cases, the characters are choosing humanity, whatever humanity they have left, over immortality.

What we don't often witness in films is the kind of suicide described in Rice's books. Mainstream filmmakers don't seem to have the guts (or the go-ahead) to allow their vampires to kill themselves for existential reasons; their suicides must be for some greater good. We see an example of this in *Let Me In*, the American remake of the Swedish vampire film *Let the Right One In*, itself based on a novel by John Ajvide Lindqvist. In the book and original film adaptation, the character of Virginia commits suicide shortly after realizing she's been turned into a vampire, by asking a nurse to open the blinds in her hospital room during the day, fully aware of what it will do to her. Lindqvist is clear about her intentions: "She wanted to turn off," he writes. As the sunlight streams in, she immediately combusts, burning to ashes. Earlier in the novel, a scene between Eli and her vampire sire explains why there are so few vampires in the world. "Most of us kill ourselves," he explains, referencing the heavy burden it is, having the dead people they drain for food on their conscience. But in *Let Me In*, the scene in the hospital room is altered: the nurse opens the blinds without instruction from Virginia, turning her into a generic vampire casualty, not someone taking her fate into her own hands.

On television, suicide by sunlight has also made appearances. On *Buffy the Vampire Slayer*, we see Angel standing on a hill waiting for the dawn. (Buffy comes to his rescue, as does nature's magic when snow appears instead of the sun.) And in the 1990s series *Forever Knight*, vampire detective Nick Knight learns that a former lover killed herself in this manner, forcing him to question his own immortality. On *True Blood*, they even give it a name: "meeting the sun." While at times it's not by choice (such as when a witch casts a spell that forces vamps out into the daylight against their will), the most dramatic occurrence is when the 2,000-year-old vampire Godric meets the sun on a hotel rooftop. In this way, he hopes to cleanse himself of his sins (namely, killing a lot of humans) and find God's forgiveness. Within seconds, his body erupts in blue flame and he is done for. Scenes like this reveal something deeper about the nature of vampire emotions and moral quandaries.

When you get down to it though, it's not really the vampires' guilt over the human victims they've bitten and bled that makes them want to give up the ghost. Or even boredom. It's the loss of those they love. As I argued earlier, love is the greatest weapon against vampires. Just like with humans, it makes them do crazy things. And just like with humans, vampires feel great pain when they outlive their loved ones. Only in their case, it's destined to happen again, and again, and again. Immortality means watching as everyone you care about gets old and dies. In the 1983 film *The Hunger* (based on a 1981 novel by Whitley Strieber), vampire Miriam Blaylock (Catherine Deneuve) can offer her lovers eternal life, but not eternal youth. While she remains vivacious, her vampire companions become elderly and desiccated, and eventually she discards them in the attic and recruits new partners. Her solution may be practical, but it's cold-hearted. Most vampires would rather die.

We've seen how in Stephenie Meyer's Twilight Saga, Edward, upon hearing the (erroneous) news that his beloved girlfriend has died, immediately decides to commit suicide. Over a girl. Because supernatural strength, the ability to read minds, eternal life and sparkle power just can't compare to the feeling of being in love. One of the best films to represent this is, rather surprisingly, the schlocky *Blacula*. When the vampire prince Mamuwalde discovers his bride is dead, he chooses to walk out into the sun, saying, "What is left for this cursed creature? His only reason for living has been taken away."

The irony here is that suicide was originally one of the reasons you became a vampire in the first place. Churches throughout Europe preached that those who took their own life would return after death as nocturnal bloodsuckers, their soul denied entry into restful paradise. It was a tool of religious control, just another way to dissuade people from killing themselves. Today, the stigma around suicide has changed, and writers of vampire stories have instead used it as a way to address the modern condition. What we've learned from their efforts is that maybe we don't need the stakes (or holy water or silver bullets), because we can simply wait for vampires to self-destruct on their own time. But that sounds agonizing, and it could take centuries. Slaying them has never been more important. Not for our own sake, but for theirs. It's an act of mercy. If you love something, particularly an undead thing, let it go. After all, in all the ways that count, it's already gone.

And now, before I let you go, a final word from the world's most infamous vampire slayer, Professor Abraham Van Helsing. In an often-edited-out segment of *Dracula*, he tells the audience before they leave the movie theatre:

> Just a moment, ladies and gentlemen! Just a word before you go. We hope the memories of Dracula won't give you bad dreams, so just a word of reassurance. When you get home tonight and the lights have been turned out and you are afraid to look behind the curtains and you dread to see a face appear at the window, why just pull yourself together and remember that after all . . . there are such things.

Acknowledgements

Once again, it is my pleasure to thank the team at ECW Press, who inspire me to make books worthy of all their hard work. In particular Michael Holmes, who said yes to publishing yet another vampire title. To Jenna Illies, Alexis Van Straten and Erin Creasey, for making me feel like a dream author. And how lucky am I to have a vampire expert for an editor? That's Crissy Calhoun, who enthusiastically and patiently handled my manuscript and, of equal importance, turned me on to the pleasures of *The Vampire Diaries*. Gary Pullin, you're a superstar. Thank you for knocking my socks off with another awesome cover. May the monsters be ever at your back.

I've read a lot of vampire books and none had such an impact on me as Anne Rice's *Interview with the Vampire*. To have Ms. Rice say nice things about my *Encyclopedia Gothica*, and then to interview her about her book *The Wolf Gift*, were highlights of the past year, of my life, and inspired me throughout this project. Thank you, Queen of Vamps.

To my colleagues at *Rue Morgue* magazine and Tomb Dragomir at Rue Morgue Radio (R.I.P.), thank you for fuelling my love for the horror genre in all its gory, gothic or goofy glories. And to Colin Geddes, who got me watching weird scary movies in the first place, without whom I would have never known about the Chinese hopping vampires, and much, much more.

ACKNOWLEDGEMENTS

Thank you Myriam Nafte for indulging my research questions about dead bodies.

David Keyes and Nancy Baker, vampire lovers and old friends, provided valuable feedback on the manuscript, as did Dr. Elizabeth Miller, Dracula expert.

Finally, this book was written during the year of the apocalypse. To my girlfriends Carol, Sharon, Andrea, Karen, Sherry, Kayla, Jovanka, Rory, Ankixa, and Sarah, eternal gratitude and much love. Here's to lucky 2013.

To everyone above, and anyone I've forgotten from lack of sleep, I'd gift you immortality if I could. Instead, I shall simply say thank you.

Selected Bibliography

Baddeley, Gavin. *Vampire Lovers: Screen's Seductive Creatures of the Night* (Plexus, 2010).

Barber, Paul. *Vampires, Burial, and Death: Folklore and Reality* (Yale University Press, 1988).

Block, Eric. *Garlic and Other Alliums: The Lore and the Science* (Royal Society of Chemistry, 2010).

Brite, Poppy Z. *Lost Souls* (Abyss, 1992).

Bunson, Matthew. *The Vampire Encyclopedia* (Crown Trade Paperbacks, 1993).

Del Toro, Guillermo and Chuck Hogan. *The Fall* (William Morrow, 2010).

Del Toro, Guillermo and Chuck Hogan. *The Night Eternal* (William Morrow, 2011).

Del Toro, Guillermo and Chuck Hogan. *The Strain* (William Morrow, 2009).

Dundes, Alan. *The Vampire: A Casebook* (University of Wisconsin Press, 1998).

Eighteen-Bisang, Robert and Elizabeth Miller. *Bram Stoker's Notes for Dracula, Annotated and Transcribed* (McFarland and Company, 2008).

Frankel, Valerie Estelle. *Buffy and the Heroine's Journey* (McFarland and Company, 2012).

Grace, Angela. *Dark Angels Revealed: From Dark Rogues to Dark Romantics, the Most Mysterious and Mesmerizing Vampires and Fallen Angels from Count Dracula to Edward Cullen Come to Life* (Fair Winds Press, 2011).

Guran, Paula, ed. *Vampires: The Recent Undead* (Prime Books, 2011).

Hamilton, Laurell K. *Guilty Pleasures* (Ace Books, 1993).

Harris, Charlaine. *Dead Until Dark* (Ace Books, 2001).

Harris, Charlaine. *The Sookie Stackhouse Companion* (Ace Books, 2011).

Jenkins, Mark Collins. *Vampire Forensics: Uncovering the Origins of an Enduring Legend* (National Geographic Society, 2010).

Joslin, Lyndon W. *Count Dracula Goes to the Movies: Stoker's Novels Adapted, 1922–2003* (McFarland and Company, 2006).

Kane, Tim. *The Changing Vampire of Film and Television: A Critical Study of the Growth of a Genre* (McFarland and Company, 2006).

Kilpatrick, Nancy, ed. *Evolve: Vampire Stories of the New Undead* (Edge, 2010).

Kilpatrick, Nancy. *The Vampire Stories of Nancy Kilpatrick* (Mosiac Press, 2000).

King, Stephen. *'Salem's Lot* (Signet Fiction, 1976).

Le Fanu, Sheridan. *Carmilla* (House of Pomegranates Press, 2012).

Lindqvist, John Ajvide. *Let the Right One In* (Thomas Dunne Books, 2007).

Matheson, Richard. *I Am Legend* (IDW Publishing, 2007).

McCammon, Robert R. *They Thirst* (Avon, 1981).

Melton, J. Gordon. *The Vampire Book: The Encyclopedia of the Undead* (Visible Ink, 1994).

Meyer, Stephenie. *Breaking Dawn* (Little, Brown and Company (2008).

Meyer, Stephenie. *Eclipse* (Little, Brown and Company, 2007).

Meyer, Stephenie. *New Moon* (Little, Brown and Company, 2006).

Meyer, Stephenie. *Twilight* (Little, Brown and Company, 2005).

Nafte, Myriam. *Flesh and Bone: An Introduction to Forensic Anthropology* (Carolina Academic Press, 2009).

Pattison, Barrie. *The Seal of Dracula* (Bounty Books, 1975).

Prothero, Stephen. *Purified by Fire: A History of Cremation in America* (University of California Press, 2001).

Ramsland, Katherine. *The Science of Vampires* (Berkeley Trade, 2002).

Ramsland, Katherine. *The Vampire Companion: The Official Guide to Anne Rice's The Vampire Chronicles* (Ballantine Books, 1985).

Rice, Anne. *Interview with the Vampire* (Ballantine Books, 1976).

Rice, Anne. *The Vampire Lestat* (Ballantine Books, 1985).

Ryan, Alan, ed. *The Penguin Book of Vampire Stories: Two Centuries of Great Stories with a Bite* (Penguin, 1987).

Skal, David J. *Hollywood Gothic: The Tangled Web of Dracula from Novel to Stage to Screen* (W.W. Norton and Company, 1990).

Snyder, Scott, Rafael Albuquerque and Stephen King. *American Vampire Volume 1* (Vertigo, 2010).

Snyder, Scott, Rafael Albuquerque and Stephen King. *American Vampire Volume 2* (Vertigo, 2011).

Snyder, Scott, Rafael Albuquerque and Stephen King. *American Vampire Volume 3* (Vertigo, 2012).

Steakley, John. *Vampire$* (Roc Books, 1990).

Stoker, Bram and Leonard Wolf. *The Annotated Dracula* (Ballantine, 1975).

Stoker, Bram. *Dracula* (Penguin, 1979).

Summers, Montague. *The Vampire, His Kith and Kin* (The Apocryphile Press, 2011).

Twitchell, James B. *The Living Dead: A Study of the Vampire in Romantic Literature* (Duke University Press, 1981).

Wellington, David. *13 Bullets: A Vampire Tale* (Three Rivers Press, 2007).

Wellington, David. *99 Coffins: A Historical Vampire Tale* (Three Rivers Press, 2007).

Wellington, David. *Vampire Zero: A Gruesome Vampire Tale* (Three Rivers Press, 2008).

Whedon, Joss and Georges Jeantry. *Buffy the Vampire Slayer: The Long Way Home* (Dark Horse Comics, 2010).

Williamson, Milly. *The Lure of the Vampire: Gender, Fiction and Fandom from Bram Stoker to Buffy the Vampire Slayer* (Wallflower Press, 2005).

Wolfman, Marv, Chris Claremont, Christopher Golden, et al. *Blade: The Vampire Slayer: Black and White* (Marvel Comics, 2004).

Wright, Dudley. *The Book of Vampires* (Dorset Press, 1987).

Yarbro, Chelsea Quinn. *Hotel Transylvania* (St. Martin's Press, 1978).

Selected Filmography

Black Sunday, directed by Mario Bava (1960).

Blacula, directed by William Crain (1972).

Blade, directed by Stephen Norrington (1998).

Blade: Trinity, directed by David S. Goyer (2004).

Blade II, directed by Guillermo del Toro (2002).

Bram Stoker's Dracula, directed by Francis Ford Coppola (1992).

Buffy the Vampire Slayer, directed by Fran Rubel Kuzui (1992).

Count Dracula, directed by Jess Franco (1970).

Daybreakers, directed by Michael and Peter Spierig (2009).

Dracula, directed by Tod Browning (1931).

Dracula A.D. 1972, directed by Alan Gibson (1972).

Dracula's Daughter, directed by Lambert Hillyer (1936).

Dracula Has Risen from the Grave, directed by Freddie Francis (1968).

Dracula 2000, directed by Patrick Lussier (2000).

The Fearless Vampire Killers, directed by Roman Polanski (1967).

Fright Night, directed by Craig Gillespie (2011).

Fright Night, directed by Tom Holland (1985).

From Dusk till Dawn, directed by Robert Rodriguez (1996).

Horror of Dracula, directed by Terence Fisher (1958).

House of Dracula, directed by Erle C. Kenton (1945).

I Am Legend, directed by Francis Lawrence (2007).

Interview with the Vampire: The Vampire Chronicles, directed by Neil Jordan (1994).

John Carpenter's Vampires, directed by John Carpenter (1998).

Last Man on Earth, directed by Ubaldo Ragona and Sidney Salkow (1964).

Let Me In, directed by Matt Reeves (2010).

Let the Right One In, directed by Tomas Alfredson (2008).

The Lost Boys, directed by Joel Schumacher (1987).

Lost Boys: The Thirst, directed by Dario Piana (2010).

Lost Boys: The Tribe, directed by P.J. Pesce (2008).

Lust for a Vampire, directed by Jimmy Sangster (1971).

Mr. Vampire, directed by Ricky Lau (1985).

Near Dark, directed by Kathryn Bigelow (1987).

Nosferatu: Eine Symphonie des Grauens, directed by F.W. Murnau (1922).

Nosferatu: Phantom der Nacht, directed by Werner Herzog (1979).

The Omega Man, directed by Boris Sagal (1971).

The Satanic Rites of Dracula, directed by Alan Gibson (1973).

Shadow of the Vampire, directed by E. Elias Merhige (2000).

Son of Dracula, directed by Robert Siodmak (1943).

Stake Land, directed by Jim Mickle (2010).

Twilight, directed by Catherine Hardwicke (2008).

The Twilight Saga: Breaking Dawn — Part 1, directed by Bill Condon (2011).

The Twilight Saga: Breaking Dawn — Part 2, directed by Bill Condon (2012).

The Twilight Saga: Eclipse, directed by David Slade (2010).

The Twilight Saga: New Moon, directed by Chris Weitz (2009).

Underworld, directed by Len Wiseman (2003).

Vamp, directed by Richard Wenk (1986).

The Vampire Lovers, directed by Roy Ward Baker (1970).

Van Helsing, directed by Stephen Sommers (2004).

Television Series

Being Human. Created by Toby Whithouse. BBC Three. 2008–2013.

Buffy the Vampire Slayer. Created by Joss Whedon. The WB/UPN. 1997–2003.

Dark Shadows. Created by Dan Curtis. ABC. 1966–1971.

True Blood. Created by Alan Ball. HBO. 2008–.

The Vampire Diaries. Created by Kevin Williamson and Julie Plec. The CW. 2009–.

Helpful Websites

Glory be to ye olde Wikipedia, and a special shout-out to www.shroudeater.com, a massive database on historical vampire accounts.

Gratitude to the fans who maintain such great wikis!

http://buffy.wikia.com

http://vampirediaries.wikia.com

http://twilightsaga.wikia.com
http://trueblood.wikia.com
http://marvel.wikia.com

Additional resources

http://www.gutenberg.org
http://www.sacred-texts.com
http://bylightunseen.net
http://vampires.monstrous.com

INDEX